700035314501

D1418625

THE FIRST JET PILOT

Isaiah
Chapter 40:31

'Those who wait for the Lord gain new strength
They will fly up with wings like eagles.'

THE FIRST JET PILOT

THE STORY OF GERMAN TEST PILOT
ERICH WARSITZ

LUTZ WARSITZ

TRANSLATION BY GEOFFREY BROOKS

Pen & Sword
AVIATION

First published in Great Britain in 2008
By Pen and Sword Aviation
an imprint of
Pen and Sword Books Ltd
47 Church Street
Barnsley
South Yorkshire
S70 2AS

Copyright © Lutz Warsitz, 2008

ISBN 978 1 84415 818 8

Translated from German by Geoffrey Brooks

The right of Lutz Warsitz to be identified as the author of this work
has been asserted by him in accordance with the
Copyright, Designs and Patents Act 1988.

A CIP record for this book is available from the British Library

All rights r   ansmitted
in any form   .otocopying,

          sy   g.

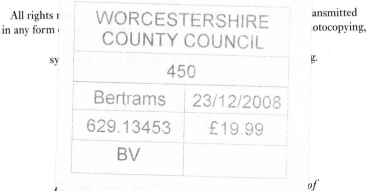

WORCESTERSHIRE
COUNTY COUNCIL

450

Bertrams	23/12/2008
629.13453	£19.99
BV	

of
Pen and Sword Aviation, Pen and Sword Maritime, Pen and Sword Military,
Wharncliffe Local History, Pen and Sword Select,
Pen and Sword Military Classics and Leo Cooper.

For a complete list of Pen and Sword titles please contact
Pen and Sword Books Limited
47 Church Street, Barnsley, South Yorkshire, S70 2AS, England
E-mail: enquiries@pen-and-sword.co.uk
Website: www.pen-and-sword.co.uk

Contents

Dedication

For my parents Doris and Erich Warsitz

Acknowledgements

I would like to remember here particularly my late father, without whom this book could not have been realized, and my late mother who supported me throughout in every respect. I thank my brother Robert for his support too: he has followed in our father's footsteps not only as a pilot but also in the technical sphere with his fine-engineering firm www.p-mec.ch. He, his wife Stefanie and son Eric have all been very important to me over the years.

When my father and I began work on the manuscript, there were two important interviews which laid the foundations: a record of the long interview from 24 October to 8 November 1952 with Paul Kettel, and the second with Harald Hein in 1979. I would like to express my gratitude to their sons, Paulpeter and Dr Karl-Heinz Kettel and their families, and especially Volker Hein, for their help: also to Mrs Hanni von Ohain who put her late husband's papers at my disposal and her son-in-law Erik Prisell.

Very great thanks also go to my cousin on my father's side Renate Stendhal, who encouraged and assisted me from her experience as an author and later edited my manuscript, leading me along the right path. I would like to thank particularly Danny Lee Nuccio (www.dannylee.org) for setting up my website www.firstjetpilot.com and Lara Donno for the cover-design of the German-language book and Mark Parret for setting up my website www.erichwarsitz.com. All photographs in this book are from my personal collection apart from those placed at my disposal and for which I am indebted to the following persons and institutions:

Karl-Ernst Heinkel, p.24 (lower), 126–29 and 133

Botho Stüwe, p. 38 and 60

Deutsches Museum – Dr Eva Mayring and Dr Wilhelm Füssl, p.121, 123 and 143

Transit Film GmbH – Daniele Guérlain, p.22, 42, 43 (middle), 46, 49, 55, 59, 62, 66 and 71 (bottom)

Adam Opel AG – Ernst-Peter Berresheim, p.21

EADS – Hans-Ulrich Willbold, p.69, 71 (upper), 72, 145-47
The National Archives (UK) – Paul Johnson p.90, 170
Swiss Museum of Transport, Henry Widler, p.13

I am very grateful to Henry Widler of the Swiss Museum of Transport for the extract from a speech by Wernher von Braun on 30 August 1971 and to the following institutions for their kind assistance:
In the UK, the RAF Museum London (Ian Thirsk), the Imperial War Museum (Matthew Lee) and the National Archives. Everywhere in the world: Traditionsgemeinschaft Alte Adler eV (Dieter Strüber), Greb & Neckermann Media Archives, Deutsche Lufthansa, Erstes Deutsches Fernsehen, Deutsches Rundfunkarchiv, Bundes Archiv, DGLR, Helmut Schubert, Strähle Luftbild, Flughafen Rostock-Laage, Museum Kummersdorf, NASA HQ History Office and Marshall Space Flight Centre, USAF Museum, Smithsonian Institute – NASM (Mark Taylor), NARA, SWR-Media GmbH, Westdeutscher Rundfunk, Militärgeschichtliches Forschungsamt, Christoph Regel, Geheimes Staatsarchiv PK, Arbeitsgemeinschaft Luftwaffe eV (Siegfried Wache), Hartmut Küper, Lufthansa Aero, Gert Ruff, Otto Lilienthal Museum, ZDF, NDR, Schweizer Fernsehen, Flugplatzgesellschaft Hangelar, Bundeswehr (Helmut Leipertz), Technik Museum Speyer, Heimatverein Neuhardenberg eV, Luftfahrttechnisches Museum Rechlin eV, FOX TV (Jan Ronca), Istituto Luce, History Channel, Doclab, Deutsche Botschaft Moskau (Dr Harald Bungarten), Deutsches Historisches Museum, Deutsches Technikmuseum Berlin, Haus der Geschichte der Bundesrepublik Deutschland, Fördergesellschaft für Luftfahrtgeschichte Köln-Bonn eV and Flygvapenmuseum (Sweden).
Hoping not to have left anybody out, I would like to thank all my relations and friends, particularly: Bruni and Edgar Neumann, Danny Nuccio, Leo Leoni, Igor and Simona Gianola, Neil Otupacca, Stephan Kaufmann, Lory Lanfranconi and Mario Cattaneo, families Krewinkel and Reinartz, Elsbeth Fahrni, Susan Tütsch, Beat Guedel, Estevere Donno and Carol Penel, Ilaria Quadri, Fabio Bossi, Johnny Frizzi, Fedra Borradori, Andrea Cavarra, Mick Taylor, Fabian Rose, Christian and Luisa Buchwald, Moreno Lenzi, 'Le Bisse di Paradiso',

Patrick and Patty Sarbach, Luca Ostini, Sergio Serafini, Demos Mariotti, Fabio Galimberti, Attilio Ghiringhelli, Mischa Pijpers, Rainer Viefhaus, the entire DHL team at Rivera, Gritli von Känel, Wilma, Marianne, Annemarie Bianchetti, Cinzia and Ivan, Ricky Gaspari and family, Guido Bizzozzero and Armando Albisetti.

Lutz Warsitz
Casa Barbara, 6992 Cimo (Switzerland)
lutz.warsitz@firstjetpilot.com

Foreword

by Lutz Warsitz

Whenever I walk near the small Lugano–Agno aerodrome at Tessin in Switzerland, I watch in fascination the take-offs and landings of aircraft of all kinds, but especially so those accompanied by the typical howl of a jet turbine. I notice that on those occasions passers-by of all ages also pause and look towards the heavens. Today of course it is not rare to see jet aircraft in which practically everybody has flown at some time or another, yet now as ever they exercise a fascination which compels one to watch them to the horizon.

Seventy years have passed since we entered the jet age. It was shortly before the Second World War when the important pioneering epoch for the development of rocket and jet engines began in which my father played a special role. As the son of a famous aviator it follows that I have inherited something of his aviator's spirit. From my childhood I felt attracted to his flying activities. When I was about age ten we made model aircraft together – not always successful ones, but they gave us a lot of pleasure.

Unfortunately I never co-piloted with my father. He did accompany me on my first flight, as passenger on an unspectacular scheduled run from Zürich to Munich, but after my first flight in a modern sports aircraft a few years ago I was only too happy to get back to *terra firma*. My great esteem for my father's achievements as aviator rose considerably, especially since he was flying purely experimental aircraft with revolutionary, untested kinds of engines, those in the He 176 in particular being very dangerous and wildly unpredictable.

At the beginning of the 1980s, for my Finals I planned to write about my father and his extraordinary life. He was very proud of this and allowed me to interview him over the period of a year. This initiated a wonderfully interesting mutual research in which he contacted his contemporaries or their descendants to obtain important material. One day he predicted: 'Perhaps you will write a book about me some day'.

In the past a lot has been written about the dawn of the rocket- and jet-age, much of it unfortunately, as my father observed, 'garnished with crap'. Much alleged is untrue and important facts overlooked. The many undignified errors and omissions relating to aviation history are partially a consequence of the outbreak of war on 1 September 1939 which followed immediately. For these reasons it became my purpose to write a book about my father, to dignify in this form for the first time his achievement in aviation and – not least – set the historical facts straight. My book permits him, as an important contemporary witness, to portray this pioneering period from his own experience and vantage point: from the technical side as engineer, from the aviation side as the first test pilot of these revolutionary 'airplanes'.

Of special value are the contributions of Walter Künzel who supported my father in his narrative. Künzel was responsible for the construction of the He 176 and He 178, and also for planning the entire test programme on the ground and in the air. Throughout this time he was my father's constant companion. It has been my aim as far as possible to quote my father verbatim from the text of my interview with him. He described his career in an ebullient manner and with some choice turns of phrase, as one can see from the text.

Before the narrative passes to my father, I would like to mention a point about the photographs. Some photographs from rare archive negatives have been copied and their quality is not up to modern standards. Nevertheless I included them because they bear irreplaceable witness to this important pioneering epoch in which my father played so great a role.

Photographs in which the contemporary military leaders and symbols of the Third Reich are shown serve the purpose of clarification and portrayal of historical scientific and military-historical events only and are not to be interpreted to suggest that I am a sympathizer of any neo-Nazi or radical-Right organization or sphere of interest. Swastikas, for example, have accordingly not been erased from the historical pictures.

At the risk of his life Erich Warsitz – as the colleague of outstanding specialists such as Wernher von Braun, Ernst Heinkel, Hans Pabst von Ohain or Hellmuth Walter – test-flew new aircraft propulsion systems which turned flight technology on its head and created those wider parameters allowing modern technology to bridge time and space.

WERNHER VON BRAUN
Swiss Museum of Transport – 30 August 1971

...To conclude my speech I should like to mention another friend in this area – Erich Warsitz. In 1939 Erich flew the world's first rocket aircraft. First of all we installed a rocket engine in a Heinkel 112, and Erich Warsitz took off in this thing from Neuhardenberg airfield 100 kilometres east of Berlin. But that was only the beginning. The same rocket motor, and another developed by the Walter firm of Kiel, were later put into

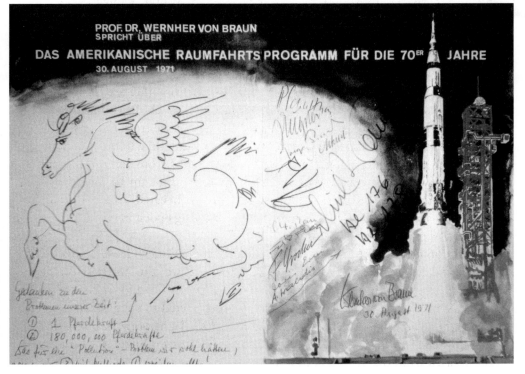

A signed programme for the meeting on 30 August 1971.

a small aircraft, the He 176, which in contrast to the He 112 had no propellor motor in the nose and only rocket propulsion. This aircraft was an absolutely crazy idea even by today's standards, so crazy that even the famous aviator Ernst Udet, then a General in the German Luftwaffe, after seeing it being flown by Erich Warsitz promptly banned him from flying it again: it was not an aircraft, he asserted, 'a thing like that without wings' could not be flown. It was some time before Erich Warsitz finally persuaded him to allow further flights. It was the first step for space travel, and played a quite important role in determining the basics, the technology and also the role of the pilot in the development of manned space travel...

HANS PABST VON OHAIN
In a letter to Doris Warsitz – 14 April 1988

I remember well my first meeting with Erich Warsitz at Peenemünde during the early summer of 1939. Heinkel had invited me to watch the second flight of the He 176. It was a great experience to see Warsitz' daring, his outstanding ability and impressive flight preparation. That evening during the grand celebrations I had the opportunity to speak briefly with Warsitz about the forthcoming test flight of the He 178.

We met several times subsequently at Marienehe where he was familiarizing himself with the He-S3B engine and its performance on the test stand, and felt sure that we were very close to the required thrust installed of 500 kg. Finally on 27 August 1939 he made the maiden flight.

It was the first flight ever of a jet aircraft. Through his enormous aviation expertise and courageous will Warsitz had introduced to the world of flying once again a completely new principle for powered flight. I witnessed his great ability on another occasion when in the presence of Heinkel's guests Udet, Milch and Reidenbach on 1 November 1939 he flew the He 178. This exhibition was highly impressive. Even if Milch did not show any emotion, I am certain that it was because of Warsitz'

display in the He 178 that shortly afterwards Heinkel received the contract to develop the He 280.

In later years I have often thought about Erich Warsitz. Even today I admire him still and am firmly convinced that through his courageous readiness to sacrifice his life if necessary, and his aeronautical-technical expertise, he contributed tremendously to the development of the jet turbine engine and rockets for manned aircraft. His image at the National Air and Space Museum, Washington DC showing him flying the first Heinkel He 178 will always bear witness to that.

I was with him for only four months altogether, from the end of June 1939 to 1 November 1939, but even though this time period was so short, it made on me an enduring impression!...

CHAPTER ONE

Flugkapitän Erich Warsitz
narrates...

It was the beautiful summer evening of 19 June 1939. The sun had just dipped below the horizon and with sunset the finest colours unfolded across the sky. I sat on the window sill with a cigarette, looked into the distance, felt the southerly wind on my cheek. Within me disquiet grew. I reflected on the only partially successful attempts to date with the bird. I was eager to get into the air with 'The Little One'. Now I took the decision. 'Tomorrow I fly her!' I would not reconsider. The die was cast. I relaxed at my writing desk, thought of my family, and revised the stages of my life which had led me to this point in time.

I was born on 18 October 1906 at Hattingen in the Ruhr. A year later my father, senior engineer Robert Warsitz, travelled alone to the Czar's Russia to set up an industrial furnace factory. The family joined him there in 1908. We lived in a fine house with a large garden. My mother, Mutz, who spoke no Russian, soon had a good interpreter in the shape of my five-year old elder brother Kurt. After my father completed his task we returned to Hattingen and around 1911 he began building a house at Grünstrasse 36. In 1913 my sister Bruni was born. It was an ideal place for us children to romp.

Erich in his early childhood.

Erich's class at the State school in 1915. He is at the extreme right in the second row from the back.

At State school my love of aircraft was noted. It displeased my father. He was summoned regularly to see the headmaster to hear complaints about my lack of attention. It seemed I preferred to make paper aircraft, fly them across the classroom and daydream. When one landed on my teacher's desk, I was given a stern warning. One day during class while gazing out of the window I saw a low flying aircraft. It landed in a field not far from the school. I watched in fascination until I could resist no longer. Brushing aside teacher and the consequences I ran from the schoolroom, jumped on my bicycle and raced to the field. Although the pilot was absent I stayed there until dark, admiring the beautiful machine. Next day I skipped school and went to the field with a paper bag full of bread rolls. I was most anxious not to miss the return of the pilot and the take-off. Despite the risk of having to go before the headmaster with my father I decided to chance it. On the third day the pilot appeared with a fuel truck to refuel his airplane. He let me sit in the cockpit, then gave me a wave, started her up and flew off. The sound of that engine was the sweetest music to my ears. I began to cry and went home sad. But one thing I knew for sure: I wanted to be a flier!

The years passed and my greatest passion became engines of all kinds. At weekends I would motor-cycle with friends to the Nürburgring to watch the motor-cycle racing. One day as a group of us was returning home from such an event something occurred which finally handed me over to the world of aeronautics. Passing the aerodrome at Hangelar we each decided to fly a circuit. I was to go first. My friends gave the pilot an inducement to loop the loop. And he did so! The passion for flying won me over and now I knew where my life belonged.

Erich had a great passion for motor-cycles and engines.

From then on I motor-cycled each weekend to Hangelar for instruction – secretly of course! So began, together with my practical tuition and technical studies, my aeronautical training as a sport flier with the Academic Aviation Group Bonn/ Hangelar for the A-2

Herchenbach
Schroedter
Horten
Ruff

Reimann
Schiller
R. Horten.

At Hangelar with the Academic Aviation Group.

licence. My flying instructor, Dr (med) Siegfried Ruff, later played an important role in rocket development. Not until I needed my birth certificate for my first examination did I have to confess everything to my parents. They were horrified! But now it was too late. Flying held me in its grip, and they understood that – they had to!

In stages subsequently came the B–1 and B–2 training at various aerodromes of the contemporary sports associations, and further training at DVS (German Commercial Pilot School) Stettin for the C–2 (land aircraft and commercial carriage of persons) and all licences for flights over the sea. Meanwhile I was awarded the major K–2 aerobatics licence, passed the blind-flying training and obtained the navigation certificate 'for short distances'.

After I had been to DVS and obtained all flying licences there, I took employment as a sporting aircraft instructor and was later transferred to the Reichsbahnstrecke (i.e. the Railway section, a cover name for long-distance flying experience, a unit concealed within the 100,000-man Weimar standing army) as flight instructor, senior flight instructor and then training leader. I had many experiences but the most important ones were to be a little later with Wernher von Braun and Dr Heinkel, who introduced me to the jet age with the He 178, and to rocket aircraft with the He 176. The most important aeronautical activities of my life had begun.

CHAPTER TWO

Rocket Fever

After the Great War when rocket fever gripped Germany, men such as Oberth, Valier, von Opel and many others were working on this relatively new idea for propulsion. For example, pilot Fritz Stamer made the world's first glider flight using a solid fuel propellant on 11 June 1928 on the Wasserkuppe mountain for the Röhn Rossitten Gesellschaft. The glider *Ente* (duck) was designed by Professor Alexander Lippisch (who later built the P-13 ramjet fighter). On 30 September 1929 Fritz von Opel made the first official rocket-assisted take-off. The flights hardly classify as the world's 'first pure rocket flights' because the aircraft were gliders by their great wingspan and did not take off under pure rocket power. *Ente* needed elasticated cables while von Opel used a rocket catapult. They were leaps into the air rather than true 'flights' but even so it was a beginning.

Fritz von Opel takes to the air on 30 September 1929.

Much associated work had been done beforehand. Experiments with rocket vehicles and sledges, for example, were part of the magic for the young Wernher von Braun, interested in astronomy since childhood. Just as aircraft fascinated me at that time, von Braun dreamed of rockets and the conquest of space. Completely infatuated with his rocket ideas, he scoured the literature and immersed himself in the thick pamphlets produced by rocket researcher Professor Hermann Oberth. In 1930 while still a young man von Braun became Oberth's assistant. At this time Oberth had developed a primitive rocket motor using liquid paraffin and liquid oxygen, and proved that liquid fuels were more efficient than powder. Later the Oberth/von Braun team and assistants became independent, conducting their experiments on an unused firing range near Berlin. This place was named *Raketenflugplatz Berlin*.

The Oberth/von Braun team at Raketenflugplatz Berlin.

The small 'association', penniless and ignored by the State, its members so hungry that they stole potatoes growing in the fields, carried out its experiments in a humble wooden shed. The experimenters were condemned as fanatics and fools. Meanwhile the Reichpost at Hannover became interested in postal rockets and the team received a few thousand marks for research. Some progress was made before a halt was called to the idea. Now the Third Reich had begun to loom. In 1929 the Army Weapons Office in Berlin wanted rockets for military purposes: in 1931 the test range at Kummersdorf took over the development of liquid fuel rockets. Hermann Dornberger, who had tested artillery munition at Kummersdorf, was very interested in rocketry, and had tried out conventional artillery rounds containing a powder propellant. Once the shell was fired, after a certain time the propellant ignited, greatly increasing the range of the shell.

Von Braun was at Kummersdorf from 1932 and developed a liquid fuel rocket in which the propellant was a high percentage of alcohol and liquid oxygen. He used this in his first experimental firing. In 1934 he fired successfully his second rocket, the A2, from the Frisian island of Borkum. After the successful conclusion of all tests, von Braun now wanted to find out how his engine would behave when installed in an aircraft in flight, a research endeavour for which he naturally required an aircraft and a lot of support, no light undertaking in that epoch. Initially financial resources were very limited. Officially, OKH (*Oberkommando des Heeres* = Army High Command) and the RLM (*Reichsluftfahrtministrium* = Reich Air Ministry) wanted nothing to do with such 'flights of fancy' as they termed them. A number of influential technical people and 'experts' in the sphere were of the opinion that an aircraft with a power unit at the rear end of the fuselage would be unbalanced and flip. Very few thought the concept was practical. Major Werner Junck at RLM offered von Braun good advice and sent him off to speak to Dr Ernst Heinkel, for whom Junck himself had flown as chief pilot and test pilot.

In the autumn of 1935 von Braun spoke to Heinkel personally, explaining about rocket propulsion, describing the experiments he had carried out and his hopes of testing a rocket engine aboard an aircraft in the air – the best being, on the advice of Major Junck, an He 112. He added that initially a fuselage would suffice for standing tests and everything should proceed in the strictest secrecy. Heinkel

Hitler surveys experiments at Kummersdorf in 1933. Werner von Braun is also in the picture standing on the left of the only soldier wearing a helmet.

listened attentively, being very interested in innovative concepts such as 'rear-thrust drive' – as the rocket and jet were called – because the

Dr Ernst Heinkel.

time was fast approaching when the traditional piston engine/propellor combination would reach its upper speed limit. With these new concepts the technical experts saw the possibilities of attaining airspeeds only dreamed of hitherto. Although everything had been tried, from souped-up engines to streamlining and modified propellors, the optimum had been reached – one could go no faster! Heinkel was also obsessed with speed and records! If he sensed that an increase in speed was possible and with it the chance of a 'Heinkel World record', he did everything he could to encourage the project. For this reason

he was immediately enthusiastic in 1936 to hear of von Braun's rocket drive, and Dr von Ohain's jet drive, and promised to give them his full support. In this area of development an enormous amount was owed to Heinkel – the little man! – who acted while others slept. This must be said!

After Heinkel had pledged his unhesitating support, he placed engineer Walter Künzel at the disposal of von Braun for the standing tests. Künzel was a capable aircraft engineer, young, accommodating and possessed of enormous energy and initiative. A little later I got to know him well. Künzel recalled,

> . . . The Heinkel works at Rostock-Marienehe had the idea of introducing liquid-fuel rocket engines into flight technology. This had been addressed seriously at an early stage. In 1934 the use of a rocket booster for fighters had been discussed. In the greatest secrecy I had carried out some research into the possibility using very optimistic values, and at the end of 1935, after being sworn to secrecy at RLM, was introduced to Dr Wernher von Braun at Kummersdorf. The sober criteria read as follows:

> (1) A liquid-fuel rocket engine of 1000 kp thrust, previously

envisaged for unmanned ballistic projectiles, built with close cooperation between rocket and aircraft engineers for testing and conversion into a reliable engine for manned flight.

(2) An aircraft – (the He 112 was already chosen) – to be fitted with this engine: because of the greater weight and the expected higher speed, such measures are to be taken as to guarantee safe flying with this engine.

Sober as the criteria for the engine may sound, these were the major difficulties to be solved:

(i) Reposition engine from the the vertical to the far more difficult horizontal thrust position.

(ii) For safe manned flight the engine had to be capable of regulation between about 40% and 100% thrust. This meant developing control instruments and additionally a suitable injection system.

(iii) It was necessary to prove that upon acceleration there would be no super-heating of the combustion chamber walls, which could lead to disaster.

From our initial conversations we concluded that the problems could only be overcome in the closest collaboration between rocket and aircraft engineers. The step forward from an engine that worked satisfactorily for unmanned 'experimental rockets' to one for manned aircraft was so great that the way was none too clear. I remember perfectly the first conversations after our return from Kummersdorf in which we stipulated that design phases were to be closely monitored and also for this new engine the most important of the safety regulations should be observed at least to the final stages.

In order to ensure the necessary close cooperation it was resolved that the designers and engineers involved in the conversion work should be resettled at Kummersdorf. This went ahead at the beginning of 1936, and we worked there in unison with Dr Wernher von Braun and his collective for over a year.

In the engine trials on the test stand the lower part of the combustion chamber always cracked. Measurements of various chambers showed that the lower part of the outer jacket was subjected to higher temperatures than the upper part. We concluded from this that because of too slow a rate of injection – which we could not improve for important technical reasons – a concentration of fuel formed on the underside of the combustion chamber which led to superheating of the wall.

This research suggested the probability that with accelerations vertical to the combustion chamber axis this problem would be worse. After consultations it was decided to build a centrifuge to investigate. This centrifuge was the first carousel with rocket drive in history. We performed a large number of acceleration tests and with an improved injection system were able to prove that the combustion chamber would resist superheating under acceleration irrespective of the spatial axis of the carrier vehicle. . .

In Wernher von Braun's first rocket motor the combustible liquids were introduced into the combustion chamber ('drive oven') and ignited there. For this purpose turbines were not used but pressure. In the engine, von Braun subjected both tanks to a pressure of between 6 to 10 atmospheres, which often resulted in their being crushed. This created an awkward situation, for this alcohol and liquid oxygen mixture was highly explosive. The centrifuge, anchored laterally to the engine, had a diameter estimated at 8 metres and was operated from a control position in the centre. Although the burn lasted only 30 seconds, in this short period a number of defects occurred: the centrifuge brake failed, the motor could not be turned off – everything was at an early stage – and so the operator ran for it! The acceleration was so great that the engine broke free, flew off and was destroyed. Everything had to be begun afresh. It was appalling!

Walter Künzel:

. . . Finding the practical proof to rebut the continuing objections of the semi-experts that the stream of combustion gases would have such a strong stabilizing effect that the aircraft would not respond to aerodynamic control surfaces caused us grave worries. Using the centrifuge we therefore made a few rather primitive attempts to provide rough proof that the aircraft would be steerable. For this purpose a known force was passed through the end of the fuselage and the deflection measured exactly. This was repeated many times with the running engine. Relying on the accuracy of the measurements with no detectable variations the results were very satisfactory. . .

In the course of the year when the first engine was finally ready, Heinkel made available an He 112 hull without wings or motor and some staff for the necessary plating work which had been bungled previously. In order to perform the standing tests in the metal fuselage, von Braun and Künzel arranged the first motor layout as follows: the oxygen tank was in front of the pilot and behind the instrumentation panel, immediately over the knees, so to speak. Behind the pilot's seat, thus at his back, was the alcohol tank, and behind that, astern in the fuselage tail, was the so-called 'oven', the actual engine. Apart from the necessary instruments and levers, everything else in the cockpit was the standard fitting.

At the end of 1936, von Braun had advanced sufficiently to undertake the first standing trials with the hull. A huge tail-fire ejected from the end of the fuselage and thus created the so-called back thrust. Then I came along.

CHAPTER THREE

Suicide Commando

At the time of my activity as a flight instructor with the *Reichbahnstrecke*, the situation at Stettin was not pleasant because the military had a finger in everything. Our commander needed his subordinates crawling to him from morning to evening. That was not how I liked things! We were still in the epoch of the clandestine *Luftwaffe*, whose existence was not made public until 1935, and we trained pilots who – in disguise – gained long distance experience on C-machines. Day in, day out over land we flew from Stettin to Hamburg, from Hamburg to Southern Germany to Breslau, and in the evening we touched down again at Stettin. This boring routine was only relieved by having the rawest novices, who brought some interest into the proceedings. Therefore I pulled out all the stops to get away. I wanted technical flying. My applications were all turned down on the grounds that too few pilots with adequate experience – particularly with a C-licence – were available.

One day I could stomach it no more. After more disagreements with our commander I decided to fly to Berlin 'over his head' and approach the department dealing with flying personnel directly. I told the competent officer, Major von Kornberg of my desperation to get into technical flying since, quite apart from the unpleasant local circumstances at Stettin, the constant flying of long-distance triangles and pupil training no longer appealed. He enquired why I had not gone through channels. I replied it was pointless because the commander would not release me. Major von Kornberg thought there might be an opportunity at Rechlin if I was agreeable. I beamed. I had heard a lot to my liking about the *Luftwaffe* Test Centre. I was ordered to return to Stettin: I would hear in due course. A few weeks later orders arrived drafting me to Rechlin. The commander was very decent about it and even had me flown there.

I embarked upon a new and extremely interesting career. The technical side was very important. Rechlin was the central test centre for the German *Luftwaffe*, and all aircraft built by German industry went there for a thorough going-over and to have weapons or special equipment installed. In short, they were made ready for the squadrons and the front. At that time in the various flight tests many young, and some not so young, pilots came to grief: they were not gambling intentionally with their lives – it was dangerous work.

Until I finally started flying rocket aircraft I worked as a test pilot and delivery pilot for all kinds of aircraft. In bad flying weather we were not required to attend at the airfield, and most would stay in their lodgings at Nierow or Neustrelitz. We made our own decisions whether to fly in fog or other adverse conditions. One morning in the autumn of 1936 the fog was so thick I could hardly see the house opposite. I decided to drive to the test centre to work on technical problems because flying was out. I returned to the Pilots' Room, being the only man of our division present. The telephone rang. 'Report to the commander immediately!' I obeyed.

"Herr Warsitz, the RLM has requested an able test pilot for a special purpose. I cannot tell you yet what it is about since it is top secret. If you say yes, I can give you a clue. I assure you it is technically a very interesting matter and you can thank your gift for technology, and flying expertise, to have merited the opportunity. Only you and Nietruch came up for consideration.'
'Why only we two, Major von Schönebeck?"
"Because you are both not married."

This was beginning to sound like a suicide mission!

"Very well," I replied, "if you tell me it is very interesting technically, I should like to give you my yes right away. I shall do it!" I waited an hour for his confirmation.

"Very well. Now I can tell you roughly what it is about. It has to do with rockets, and some flight tests are involved. Where and what I have no idea. I hope on your next visit you will give me more details, because I am intrigued. Fly to Berlin tomorrow and report to Oberst Junck at the RLM Technical Office."

Next day in his office Junck greeted me with, "Wonderful to see you, Warsitz!" To the extent that he was himself in the picture, Junck provided me with an explanation of the secret work being done before sending me to see engineer Pauls, the consultant responsible for rocket motor development in the RLM engine division. Pauls told me what he knew, and informed me that I would be taken to Kummersdorf next morning.

Kummersdorf was heavily guarded and fenced off. We drove over the terrain, through a forest, along a sandy track and stopped before a lowly barrack hut in a wood. Inside the hut the cigarette smoke was so thick I could barely see the five or six men seated at a table. At my entry they all rose, and the first to make himself known was a certain Wernher von Braun. After introducing me to the others he said, "We already know, Herr Warsitz, you are the pilot who will be working with us on a new concept!" At that he launched into an hour-long dissertation on the enterprise: his rocket, his ideas and everything he had done so far. Then he broached the theory.

I found it all fascinating, but von Braun was so deeply into the subject and such a gifted scientist that his lecture to a layman such as myself was rather wasted. He scribbled formulae and mathematical equations on the blackboard. For a while I nodded my understanding and said yes, yes, before finally admitting, "My dear Herr von Braun, this is all Greek to me. What is it you are actually proposing to do here?" In response he revealed that he wanted to test his rocket aboard an aircraft in flight. Concluding his monologue he decided to familiarize me next with a test-stand run, showing me the corresponding apparatus in the aircraft. On the way to the sand trench, where for the purpose Heinkel's wingless hull had been stationed, von Braun led me to a sort of workshop – old fashioned and primitive which housed a great pile of torn and contorted containers. In von Braun's temporary absence a mechanic told me that they were 'ovens' or 'casseroles'. These terms meant nothing to me, and I said so. He snapped back, "Sometimes we call them combustion chambers."

"And how did they get into that condition?"

"They exploded. And if you are unlucky, Herr Warsitz, and do not take great care, you will finish up on top of them."

Von Braun had now returned and saw me looking at the heap. He said the containers had been "specially shaped for materials testing purposes".

"For what kind of materials testing? For steel and light metals you have the manufacturer's certificate," I replied. He turned his back at once and refused to be drawn any further on the matter. I accompanied him and the whole team to a large sandy trench deep in the woodland. To one side was a concrete wall, apparently as splinter protection. Behind it was the control stand from where ignition was started remotely. Remotely, because the rocket engines tended to explode at this stage. The engine 'oven' had once run for thirty seconds on the stand before something went wrong: as a rule it would finish up in shreds on the heap.

After von Braun had explained the machine and engine to me he said, "So, now we are going to show you a run on the stand. I will do it for you." He took his seat in the pilot's position of the hull and instructed me, "You stay close by me, stand on the wing root so that you can see what I am doing." He exuded confidence as if the procedure was totally mundane, and exchanged any number of remarks with the various crew posts. The engine was turned on at the precise moment when the pressures in the liquid oxygen and alcohol containers respectively reached a specific level: not until then did he operate some levers in a particular order for the purpose. Once started it could not be stopped, neither if on fire or when it exploded. If he got the levers wrong it blew up, and when it blew the splinters whizzed everywhere!

I knelt on the wing root and watched von Braun at the instrument panel. He worked innumerable levers, switches and push-buttons, none of which meant anything to me, and so controlled the rise in pressure. The came ignition! A thud shook the hull, and a strange stutter began at the tail. More pressure in the tanks, more workings of various levers, a regulating of certain instruments and then, after about 60 seconds, he counted, "Three, two, one...." Boom! A deafening noise!

Until then I had experienced many thorny situations in flying but this – this gripped me, God knows, still more, this thunder, this gigantic noise, and always the air pressure which surrounded one and which one felt forward in the cockpit region – standing up! When it started, the full power of the rocket thrust tugged at the machine's anchorage so that I had to grip the flange and play the strong man, otherwise the pressure would have ripped me off. I was extraordinarily impressed – enchanted. After a few seconds I glanced towards the tail and saw the blue-white tongue of fire three to four metres long. Its temperature was over 2000°C, and looked like a huge spot weld with a long flame. 20 or 30 metres behind us was the wall of the sandy trench with its 10-mm thick steel plates two metres square to prevent the sand swirling in the air. These heavy plates had been left loose. Looking back I noticed how the pressure waves whirled them one after another into the air like autumn leaves, giving some impression of the power involved here. After thirty seconds the theatre came abruptly to its end. I murmured: 'Thank God!' People sheltering behind stout trees and the thick concrete wall came running out. Von Braun looked at me and I thought, 'Fly a thing like that? What have I let myself in for?'

They were all pleased with this successful test, especially having von Braun in the cockpit and myself alongside, for previously von Braun had always ignited the motor from the observation post with its protective concrete wall thirty to forty metres away. It was actually the first time that the motor had been started from the cockpit, and naturally everybody had been praying for it not to explode! Von Braun and Künzel had agreed beforehand,

> 'When the pilot arrives we must not put him behind the concrete wall under any circumstances. We must make him confident of the engine from the outset or he will have doubts – and then it will go awry!'

That was quite right. When one stood behind the wall, whose purpose was to protect against metal splinters should the motor explode, one was overwhelmed by the trembling and shaking of the air, by the air pressure, the noise and the shock waves. If on the other hand one sat in the cockpit or stood close by, it was only half as bad. And they knew that. They had told themselves: "If he stands just once behind the wall, then he is intimidated for always. He has to be on the machine." When the test had concluded von Braun asked me: "What do you say now?". I was so captivated I could hardly speak. I replied: "I cannot say anything, Herr Doktor. At the moment, I find myself speechless."

"Yes," he said, "It may of course be a bit strange to you. You will have to get used to it. But it is a completely harmless affair, we have made any number of experiments and it is considered almost reliable, the whole apparatus." I was left believing what he said, but the time would come when I had the physical evidence that it was anything other than reliable!

Dusk had fallen. Von Braun invited Künzel and myself to accompany him into Berlin. I accepted with pleasure, hoping to learn more about the project. Upon seeing his car I was taken aback – surely this wreck could not be his automobile! Only half a rear fender, a front mudguard terribly mauled and buckled, the vehicle unwashed for many years. An old 6-cylinder Opel. Von Braun got into the driver's seat, Künzel sat in the back. The right-side passenger door was a little ajar. I wondered at his effrontery in taking such a machine on the road but made no remark as a matter of courtesy. The interior of the car was as poorly maintained as the exterior. There were technical magazines on my seat. As I made to remove them, von Braun said, "It's best to leave them where they are, but if you'd rather know why, just lift them up." I shifted the mountain of magazines aside and a large spiral spring bounced up. I replaced the magazines. I wanted to close the door but the strap was absent. "Ach, the catch is broken and the strap fell off," von Braun said. From below his seat he produced a cord. "Tie up the door with this!"

"And what shall I attach it to?"

"To the window winder."

"There is no window winder on this door."

"Ach ja," he replied, "we had to take it off yesterday for use in a test, that is why." At that he got out, bound the cord tightly and tossed the loose end through the glass-less open window with the comment, "Improvisation is half of life."

"I do hope your rocket does not need bits of cord."

After fastening the cord around the steering column von Braun climbed in and we drove off. At a dangerous crossroads behind Kummersdorf a car came at us suddenly. Von Braun ignored it and maintained speed. A tangible jolt told us we had collided. Speechless with shock I looked at von Braun. He shook his head and said quietly, "Gentlemen, that was no more than a mere glancing blow."

In Berlin we parked on the Kurfürstendamm and had ragout stew in a restaurant while discussing technical matters. Von Braun then suggested we should go on to the 'Aschinger'. This surprised me a little, but when he ordered stuffed cabbage and the waiter already seemed to know the preferences of the diner, all became clear. Giant portions were served up and von Braun wolfed his down. Afterwards we went to the popular 'Zigeunerkeller' where the waiter brought a magnum of champagne we had not ordered and which cost nothing. Prinz zu Biesterfeld, later the German consort of Queen Juliana of the Netherlands, was the major spender of the night and covered our bill amongst others. Thus this nocturnal crawl continued until six in the morning and passed in cheerful chatter not specifically about rockets or the planned test flight.

In the best of spirits we returned to von Braun's car. Near the Gedächtnis Church he stopped and turned to me. "Are you with us and will you test the rocket in the air?"

"Yes!" I answered. "Then, Warsitz, you will be a famous man. And later we will fly to the moon – with you at the helm!" He used the 'Du' familiar pronoun and said that I was now a member of 'the conspiracy'. This had to be marked by a bet. He proposed circling the Gedächtnis Church three times against the traffic flow without the police noticing. 'OK, give it a go,' Künzel and I agreed. Close to completing the third circuit a whistle – Police! Stop! With his slick talk and charm von Braun pacified the gendarmes and kept them talking until six struck, when the matter was out of their hands because their shift ended at six. They came for a drink in a nearby tavern, but preferred to use teacups for their Schnapps. I was won over that night for the flight testing by the friendship of Wernher von Braun. I told myself that one would go through fire for a man with such verve, class and humour in his dealings with people, and so many equations is his head – he would achieve his goal!

I returned to Rechlin and informed Major von Schönebeck under a pledge of secrecy. The RLM had made me promise faithfully never to divulge any of it to anyone. A few days later I was given accommodation at Kummersdorf. I built up my friendship with von Braun very quickly. He was not only a fantastic person but also had tireless energy and tremendous visionary ideas. Von Braun and I both worked around the clock. His ideas and ambition had gripped me so tightly that for the time being nothing else mattered. I had overcome my first doubts, and upon spending time in Berlin after my first visit to Kummersdorf I thought: 'I have done a lot of dangerous things in flying, and everything finished well. If I have to take this bird and gear up and I survive that, then I can do whatever I want in life, for no ill can ever befall me!'

I had of course taken into account that such a venture would no go absolutely smoothly, but the concept fascinated me!

The entire Club then working at Kummersdorf numbered 25, and I was the 26th. Walter Künzel, just as possessed as von Braun and I, was also a one hundred percenter. We formed a trio, in character equally stainless, which remained inseparable to the end. I noticed very soon that what von Braun had said to me on the first day was not even remotely true. One either suffered a definite dizziness in successful test stand runs or the engine blew up and the metal splinters flew. Test followed test, hardly any of them going off without a hitch. Since it was obviously dangerous, von Braun returned to remote ignition. We were still working with the He 112 wingless hull.

OKH had gradually developed an interest. Until then we had not dared invite a team to come and witness the apparatus in action because of the perpetual risk of its exploding. Certain gentlemen were interested in it, the work had cost a pretty penny so far, and finally the Army Weapons Office turned up. They saw the entire hull disintegrate on the test stand. Heinkel had understanding for such failures and gave us another hull in which a new DIY engine was installed for the next test. The hull was secured with ropes and cables and blocked off forward. The aft section did not rest on the tail wheel but was fixed horizontal for the tests because the fluid level was important. In the initial flight tests the rocket motor would not be switched on at take-off but while in level flight in the air.

The thrust was measured with many strange instruments and the results charted. After each test the engineers would add to and evaluate diagrams for temperature measurement, fuel consumption per individual tank and overall, and so on. For the later flight trials Heinkel would make available an airworthy He 112 into which we fitted an additional motor: one tank ahead of the cockpit, the other behind it, further aft the motor and at the tail the chamber. The piston engine, all flight controls and the outer structure we left unchanged. Some of the preparatory work and new installations were carried out at Kummersdorf.

The Heinkel He 112.

After months of tireless endeavour it was now time to find an airfield where we could begin the actual flight testing in conditions of secrecy, limiting the risks. RLM told us: 'It cannot be done on any existing aerodrome for lack of secrecy, find yourself some other place or field.' Künzel and I took a Heinkel Kadett, which Heinkel had put at our disposal, and scoured the outskirts of Berlin. We wanted to remain close to the capital if possible to maintain close links to the *Luftwaffe* centres and to everybody essential for the performance of the tests. From the air we spotted a large, interesting field, flew back and drove there in a car. This was Neuhardenberg, about 70

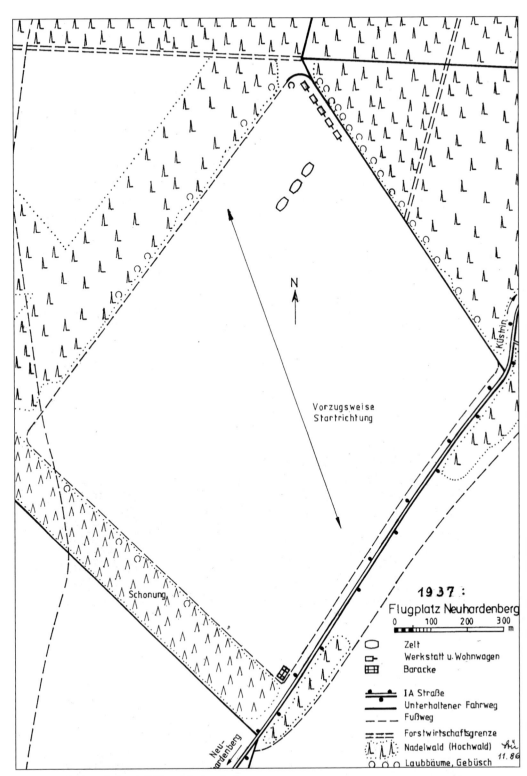

A plan of the airfield at Neuhardenberg.

kilometres east of Berlin, a very large field belonging to the estate of Graf Hardenberg. It was a designated *E-hafen*, an auxiliary airfield in the event of war. We considered it suitable for our purposes and advised the RLM accordingly. It was then allocated to us.

We experienced fresh difficulties. The field lacked any kind of structure. Obviously we could not run tests from an open field with no facilities, and so I flew to Rechlin to organize a workshop convoy. Rechlin had one of these, consisting of some funfair caravans fitted out as mechanical workshops with office, sleeping and kitchen trailers. When this rolled into our field at Neuhardenberg we put it into one corner and erected some large tents to house the aircraft. Next we commandeered the strongest local guard unit to protect the airfield, emphasis being put on the need for the strictest adherence to the regulations regarding secrecy. We settled in at Neuhardenberg in the spring of 1937 after making all necessary preparations for the tests. We had an airworthy He 112, an He 112 wingless hull and all required instrumentation. Tests resumed using the hull.

The tents that housed the aircraft.

The workshop convoy. Workshop, sleeping and kitchen trailers.

In parallel with the He 112 fitted with the von Braun motor, much more had been started: the RLM had suddenly developed an interest in rocket boosters which fitted below the wings of heavily loaded bombers to assist take-off from small aerodromes and auxiliary fields with short runways. Once in the air the containers would be discarded by parachute for re-use. This development was worked on by the Walter firm of Kiel.

Hellmuth Walter had concentrated on rocket boosters. He used a different rocket fuel to von Braun: whereas the latter's engines were powered by alcohol and liquid oxygen, Walter engines had hydrogen peroxide and calcium permanganate as a catalyst. Von Braun's engine used direct combustion and created fire, the Walter devices hot vapours from a chemical reaction, but both created thrust and provided high speed.

There now began a very close cooperation with the Walter factory. The first standing trials of their boosters were held at Neuhardenberg using an He 111E placed at our disposal by heinkel. Now RLM had given Hellmuth Walter a contract to build a rocket engine for the He 112, and for test purposes he had also received an He 112 hull to make standing tests. With this a demonstration was to be provided for RLM observers at Kiel to raise the mysterious veil shrouding rocket development. I was to be in the cockpit and ignite the engine from my seat, and not by remote control. The preparations at the Walter factory were completed and once the technical lecture was over the gentlemen withdrew behind the concrete wall.

Walter's senior engineer, Bartelsen, who was also at Neuhardenberg in 1937, told me shortly before the demonstration, "Ach, you know what? We should remote-ignite it."

"Don't foul it up," I retorted, "you can't give these people the impression that not only does it look dangerous, but we actually *believe* it's dangerous. I must be in the cockpit." Bartelsen seemed to have some kind of premonition. Putting me under increased pressure he urged, "Don't do it, come on, do me a favour. I don't know."

"Is there something not right with the thing?"

"No, nothing has changed, all our tests went off like clockwork, but this demonstration would be just the right time for something terrible

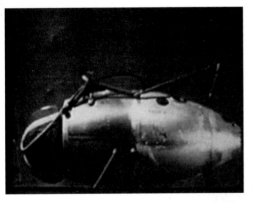
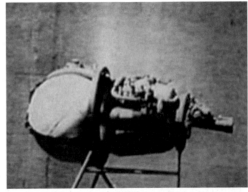

Various views of Hellmuth Walter's rocket booster.

to happen." These were the words which saved my life. I gave in and went behind the concrete wall. When the remote ignited the engine there was a terrible explosion. A deathly hush followed. Smoke filled the whole factory, through it some cries were heard: two mechanics had been sprayed with hydrogen peroxide and the water hoses were not working. The chemical smarted appallingly if taken in the face. At last the water came through and the flames were extinguished. By the time we got to the aircraft the vapour had dispersed. The calcium permanganate had exploded in the catalyst tank, destroying the inboard installation. The aircraft had outward damage only at the tail, not serious, but the tank of hydrogen peroxide ahead of the pilot's seat had burst, the catalyst had mixed with the fluid causing another explosion which had destroyed the tank. I climbed into the hull for a closer look at the damage. A fragment of the forward tank about the size of a fist had passed through the pilot's seat and the rear bulkhead like a shell fragment. I recalled Bartelsen's mysterious premonition.

The He 111E used for early experimental flying with the rocket boosters.

Had I been seated there the fragment would have passed through my chest.

My miraculous escape faded into insignificance compared to our major worry. The gentlemen from RLM and OKH hammered it into us continuously: 'Make sure that there is not the least problem. The tiniest thing, Warsitz, and our whole development is for the chop'. Later, during the war, there was less call for caution: all kinds of mishaps occurred and many men lost their lives as a result of them. But in the early days caution was fundamental. All the same, the He 112 was fitted with the Walter engine system in the meantime and joined von Braun's He 112 at Neuhardenberg. However, the first aircraft to take off from there was the He 111.

CHAPTER FOUR

Flight Tests
at Neuhardenberg

By the early summer of 1937 the Walter take-off boosters were so far advanced that I could test fly an He 111 with them. Walter Künzel flew with me – he refused to be left behind! I wanted no mechanics aboard so that if anything went seriously wrong only two men had to jump for it. The weather was highly unfavourable with cloud cover at 1000 metres. Normally such maiden flights, in which there is a possibility that the aircraft might blow up and the aircrew rely on their parachutes deploying, are made at several thousand metres. 'Speed and altitude are half your salvation' is an old flying motto!

Erich with Walter Künzel.

For the first flight we did not invite
the club but kept it dark. Since there
were some new Heinkel mechanics
around, the entire technical team at
Neuhardenberg now numbered 35 men.
The aircraft held its course straight and
true and climbed phenomenally with the
added thrust of two 300-kg rockets. The
angle at which they were fitted made the
aircraft tail-heavy however. The airspeed
wanted, so far as I remember, was 250

*A rocket-assisted take-off by the
HE 111.*

kms/hr, but that was not a decisive factor. The booster rockets had
their 30-second burn and we made a smooth landing.

Walter Künzel:

'. . .The first flights gave us a few surprises, however: we had
taken into account the force moment surrounding the transverse
axis which developed when the rockets fired, but at the same
time the airflow around the wings was changed to such a degree
by the rocket jet-stream below the wings that we almost achieved
a reversal of the rudder effect. . .'

Our work was systematic and I made several hundred flights with the
rocket boosters at Neuhardenberg. I recall only one adverse incident.
When about to rotate the rockets dislodged. I avoided catastrophe by
cutting the gas and spun to a stop. These rockets could be turned off,
in contrast to earlier models.

RLM was very enthusiastic about this development, particularly
because the initial test programme had been relatively trouble-free.
Within a short time we began to set records for heavyweight take-offs.
RLM had given aircraft manufacturers the following specification: A
standard aircraft – such as the He 111 – had to reach 20 metres
altitude with a take-off run of 600 metres. The He 111E could meet
this condition with its normal all-up weight and full load totalling ten
tonnes. Now they wanted an increase in payload, but a standard He
111 of 13 tonnes with standard engines and all equipment would not
lift off because the additional payload cut its speed below that
necessary for take-off. A few years before I had made similar tests

with the He 111 at Rechlin on Lake Müritz in a winter when the lake was frozen over and could be used as an 'airfield'. Although we covered several kilometres at full throttle the aircraft would not come unstuck even though the weight was below 13 tonnes.

Now we would try it with the rocket boosters. We loaded up good old AMUE – the poor craft had gone through heaven and earth with us – to the limit, asking the uttermost of the frame by building into the fuselage additional water tanks and then filling the space with eight cement bombs and sandbags. Everything we did, I must confess, had no approval! The weight was increased gradually to the 13 tonnes of the specification, and what had only been possible with ten tonnes could now be done with over 13 tonnes using the rocket assist at take-off.

Since the burn time for the He 111 was only 30 seconds, we learned from experience that the booster rockets should not be ignited at the moment when we gave the engines full throttle and the machine rolled, but we should allow the 'furniture waggon' to run the first twenty to forty metres under her ordinary engines before igniting the rockets. This was because the time required to reach the 40-metre mark from a standing start was too long: we had plenty of fuel for the engines but only 30 seconds burn time for the rockets. If they were ignited at the start of the run, just as the aircraft was lifting off, or had just come free, the 30 seconds was up, the rocket fuel ran out, and then one sagged!

The He 111 always sagged. Once I reached 20 metres altitude with 13 tonnes and shut off the rockets to see how she would respond. The aircraft sank two or three metres with the weight and hung in the air like a ripe plum – the engines were basically too weak for the load: initially two DB 600s, later two DB 601s were installed. Then I flew a kilometre horizontal to maintain speed, held her low near the ground, passed over the neighbouring field and went slowly into a steep ascent. On the first flights I would quickly jettison the water ballast once in the air in order to avoid risks on landing. Later I abandoned the practice because the undercarriage had to be able to take the full weight. The good old Heinkel made it! Heinkel's machines had very strong legs and I believe this was a decisive factor in all our tests. We tried all kinds of different weight configurations which would have weakened another manufacturer's aircraft to the

The rocket experimental flight team pose in front of the He 111. Erich and Walter Künzel on the extreme right.

extent that even the standing tests would not have been successful with them. Everybody was convinced of that fact. For this reason we were very enthusiastic about Heinkel aircraft, the He 112 was the right machine for the basic rocket-aircraft tests as was the He 111 for the take-off tests.

We had a long series of successful tests, and then came a thorny situation. Because of the wind direction I was forced to take-off a 12-tonner from the field with woodland ahead. For reasons unknown at the time one of the rockets failed after I was in the air and approaching the woods. The aircraft performed an about-face of 180°! I had one booster rocket still burning. Since this was between the engine and wingtip it enlarged the lever effect to the fuselage horizontal axis. My correct course of action was to tread down the opposite rudder pedal heavily, but that would have lost me some speed which is, as is known, very dangerous during take-off! Since I could not permit myself lateral thrust, I was forced to shut down the second rocket. After disengaging this rocket I was climbing with 12 tonnes and had to keep gaining height to clear the wood with the standard engines. I managed it – just – the wheels clipping the treetops!

Künzel and Anton Beilmann, my flight engineer who flew the whole programme with me, also succeeded in overcoming ticklish situations with an steely calm. Beilmann was present at the He 176 project from the very beginning and participated at all my flights. After reporting the string of successful take-offs with the He 111, we made the first demonstrations for the RLM brass. Not the top men, but the men in the Technical Office below Junck who made the decisions, a number of gold braid generals of the Admin Staff who handled the finances, and those who needed to know. What excitement at the start! By now I had reached a stage of confidence where I could try something showy but risky. I decided to make a cavalier take-off without payload – something extraordinarily impressive for a bomber aircraft. I roared up the runway with the normal engines and

The He 111 makes a demonstration take-off with rocket assistance for the RLM.

after a longer delay than usual fired the rockets and left the ground immediately. I took the greatest care to climb as nearly vertical as possible. It made a fantastic impression, especially with all the clouds of smoke billowing out astern. Theatrical admittedly, but the effect on the spectators was startling!

Dr Heinkel, who had been present on previous occasions and had witnessed some of the rocket-assisted flights, also watched this exhibition flight. The boosters were tried out on other aircraft besides the He 111. The Ju 88 was the mass-produced bomber of the time and was developed for rocket-assisted take-offs, as was the entire He 111 series. They were fitted with the necessary installations for the rockets irrespective of whether they would be required for the operational work in which the aircraft would be involved. I did the entire Ju 88 programme of tests, but later at Peenemünde. At Neuhardenberg only Heinkel types were available. In connection with that, at the outbreak of war, so called rocket-booster squads were formed by the *Luftwaffe*, equipped with all necessary ground equipment, and a certain number of rocket-booster companies were attached to each squadron, as I will describe later.

Von Braun also worked on the development of rocket boosters, but major difficulties put him behind schedule so that at Neuhardenberg all He 111 tests used only Walter rockets. Von Braun's 500-kg thrust rockets were not ready until 1938. He evaluated the experience gained with the rocket boosters, applying it to the rocket-engine project with the He 112, but these tests did not all go well. Work on his He 112, the flight version, in which the experimental engines had first been installed at Kummersdorf, was terminated, and a programme of standing tests begun. For safety reasons these were initially remote-fired and only later ignited by myself from the pilot seat. We considered it progress if two consecutive standing tests went off without a hitch. The most common defect was the combustion chamber splitting due to pressure build-up. As regards complete safety, in the few months remaining there was no time for such niceties.

The rocket motor had meanwhile been made somewhat safer. After we had two relatively good tests behind us I said, "Now let's call a halt. It has succeeded twice, we do not need to keep on and on, besides there is no more time to lose". I could not convince the others. Künzel, responsible for the aircraft and its installations was not happy with the latter and the same went for von Braun and his rocket motor.

"There's no point in further delay, we must press on," I argued. They both agreed to do no more that day, since it was late afternoon,

The He 111 with Braun's 500-kg thrust rocket.

and insisted: "One more standing test early tomorrow and if that goes well you can risk a flight!"

Next morning the aircraft was made ready for a standing test. I got into the pilot's seat and switched on. There was a terrible explosion and I found myself four metres from the aircraft amongst pieces of seat and control gear. This time not only the combustion chamber had split, the whole fuselage seemed to have ripped apart. The explosion had catapulted me out laterally, but I was unharmed. As I stood up, everybody came running. We were now no further forward than we had been many weeks previously. Our disappointment was enormous. A demonstration of the He 112 with the von Braun rocket promised to RLM had to be cancelled.

Upon receiving our report Heinkel said very little. Because time was pressing he was not interested in failures. Only going forwards was important, and he was approachable. If we needed anything we only had to ask. Through *Luftwaffe* channels on the other hand we did not wish to go! How long it took through them, and who knew with what outcome, for there were many at that time, highly placed military men with little appreciation of technology, poised to strike out the entire development at the slightest excuse. Heinkel's support was decisive for the whole development. And so he gave us another airworthy He 112 which we had to convert for our purposes: this took a few weeks.

After two or three consecutive tests without mishap I spoke out again: "Now let's put an end to all this testing on the ground – the next will be flown!" Next day the weather was very unfavourable, cloud base 500 metres. The others were opposed to my flying. "Nevertheless I shall fly, get the aircraft ready and no more objections!" I said sternly, I just wanted to get it over with. As with the He 111 we did not want to chance starting straight off with the rocket. Our plan was to take off under normal engine power, climb to altitude, increase speed, level off, ignite rocket. While warming up the aircraft engine, von Braun's rocket was made ready. The tanks had been filled with the rocket fuel and I now had to wait for the pressure to build up, the natural evaporation of the liquid oxygen created the pressure we needed in the tanks. Once this had run its course the motor had to be started 'Now, for heaven's sake' or we had to abandon the attempt. The rocket motor had to be switched on at a precise time or it would malfunction or explode. I had everything worked out for the He 112 flying laboratory. It took ten minutes for a pressure between 5 and 6 atmospheres to build up, when I would switch on.

I took off with the standard engine, climbed to about 450 metres below the cloud base and made a circuit. I had the pressure. Over the airfield I throttled to about 300 kms/hr and operated my profusion of levers. With a tangible jolt the aircraft shot forward. 'Shot forward' is perhaps an exaggeration. One would not expect that from 300 kgs thrust with an aircraft the weight of the He 112 (1680 kilos empty). All the same I felt a noticeable jerk forwards despite my current airspeed and within seconds I was at 400 kms/hr, of that I am certain. Seconds after engaging the rocket motor, quantities of smoke and gas began to enter the cockpit. I raised my goggles, worn for emergency, from my throat to my eyes, forced open the canopy – the gases irritated my eyes so much that I had them squeezed shut. From the corner of my eye I saw flames behind me in the fuselage, the details I could not make out. My speed was increasing, my rocket motor aflame. I shut down the Junkers Jumo engine to keep my speed level because I lacked altitude. Now I was flying under rocket power alone. A very high temperature accompanied the gases coming into the cockpit. This had all happened within a few seconds, of course. I could not turn off the rocket and had to let it run its 30-second burn phase. It was getting ever hotter forward. Bale out!

I unbuckled my straps rapidly and was about to get up to jump clear when I noticed that by shutting down the piston engine I had lost altitude to only 200 metres. The risk of using the parachute at this height was great. Lose height and get her down somewhere! I told myself. I lost more altitude by side-slipping without increasing speed. Almost at ground level I crossed the airfield boundary, but had no time to get the wheels down. Suddenly the 30 seconds was up, the rocket cut out and I landed wheels-up on the airfield at the same instant. I jumped clear and ran! Scarcely had I done so than the aircraft was afire. The pumps and ambulance drove up – every kind of vehicle naturally at readiness for such emergencies – and extinguished the flames.

Von Braun, Künzel and all the others came running, horrified. What was the cause? The tanks with aviation spirit in the wings were intact – the rocket was the problem. Here is what happened. The rocket motor in the hull leaked at numerous places causing a dangerous flammable mixture to gather. To guard against this we had introduced ventilation slats fitted through the fuselage just behind the cockpit. This created an airflow internally during flight preventing the gases accumulating and sweeping them astern where they were expelled. By mistake the vents had been installed to face the wrong way so that in flight there was no sternward flow and the fumes and jet flame were sucked forward into the cockpit. The crash-landing had not been necessary because the rocket motor had functioned correctly. The combustion chamber had a hair-fracture, however, through which the rocket fuel came out in a fine spray and naturally burned. Therefore not only the gases were sucked forward but also the heat from the flames in the fuselage.

From the ground the observers were mystified as to why I had decided to land with the undercarriage up. They had no means of knowing that some of the tail flame was roasting me in the cockpit and were naturally surprised to see the cockpit canopy fly off and a rapid descent, followed by my sprint to safety after the aircraft slid to a halt on the field. The gases burning in the fuselage seriously damaged the rear section of the aircraft, and I suffered a murderous dizzy spell, but otherwise my belly landing was the correct decision.

If in order to gain time to lower the undercarriage and make a reasonable landing I had flown a circuit using the Junkers engine – which was quite possible since the flight characteristics of the aircraft had not been changed by the addition of the rocket motor – a serious problem would probably have arisen as I approached the airfield at low altitude. As we established later, gas escaping the combustion chamber through the side was burning at a high temperature and had seared the aileron rods and burned three-quarters through. Making the kind of sudden rudder movement which would have been necessary during a tight circuit, the aileron rod would probably have come free causing my aircraft to nose-dive into the ground from a few metres' altitude.

All's well that ends well! We set up a tripod, raised the aircraft with a crane to lower the undercarriage, then pushed the machine into a marquee. The only damage was a few dents. The engine cooling unit was also knocked about somewhat but the rocket was still not right and so we didn't cry too much over the cooler.

This first flight aborted at the beginning of June 1937. The first rocket flight of the He 112 had hardly met our wildest dreams and hopes. It was a failure except that it enabled our superiors to prove to the doubters and critics that an aircraft was indeed capable of being flown under thrust from the rear. It had really been the purpose of von Braun's rocket motor, and all tests with the He 112, to prove that very point. It was never our intention to break records, or design tactics with this first type, or fly anything more.

We returned to our office caravan. Naturally there was a lot of discussion. We cooperated to compose the report required for RLM and the Luftwaffe departments, and had got to the point where the hot gases had entered the cockpit.

"How should we describe that?" von Braun asked.

I said, "Well, quite simply, hot gases reached the cockpit seat." Despite the serious matter in hand, all burst into laughter, although it took me a few seconds to see the double meaning. We phrased it differently and advised RLM and OKH in advance by telephone of the text of the report.

It was of course a stroke of double luck that I had come out of this particular flight unscathed. If, as I was intending, I had parachuted down and the machine had crashed all the enormous amount of work which had been put into it from all sides would have been lost and the justifiable fear would have arisen that the project might have been cancelled by higher authority. That was not the case, and we were given the go-ahead to proceed at the same tempo.

Next day I had to report in person at RLM and was then admitted to a Berlin hospital for an operation to relieve considerable suffering from an injury I had sustained in 1936. In a crash I had torn the duodenum. It could not be stitched and the surgeons deliberated whether to seal the 4-cm long tear with a silver pin. If they had done so it would have meant the end of my flying career because I would have had to avoid high speeds and great physical exertion. In the end they cauterized it and I was able to leave hospital three weeks later in excellent shape. I have never since experienced any problem with it and remain eternally grateful to Dr Bock at Berlin's Gertrauden Hospital.

Subsequent flights in the He 112 at Neuhardenberg were made with the Walter rocket and not von Braun's. In principle both worked much the same way but used a different fuel mixture and different systems of combustion. The Walter motor was simpler to maintain and not so dangerous for pilot and machine – more reliable in every respect!

Walter Künzel:

> . . .The propulsion system known humorously as the "cold Walter process" had great advantages for the experimental flights we were making. It had been designed originally for its simplicity and safety. The disadvantage lay in the relatively high specific consumption, though this was not critical for test flights. The difference in specific consumption between the two engines (5.5×10 (to the power-3) kp/kg/sec – von Braun) and (8.5×10(to the power-3) kp/kg/sec – Walter) and the resulting differences in temperature show immediately why the von Braun motor was so difficult to control. The latter worked at a combustion chamber temperature of about

Experiments underway on the He 112 fighter.

> 2000°K, the Walter process at only 750°K, which limited the problem area. A series of fundamental problems had been solved as the result of development work on the von Braun rocket motor and so the tempo of the research could be substantially accelerated. . . .

We carried out the whole series of tests with the He 112 fighter. Its flights with the Walter rocket required special clothing for the pilot. When this high percentage hydrogen peroxide fuel came into contact with clothing material the latter acted as a catalyst, dissolving and burning. Accordingly the RLM development division was given the task of designing a protective suit. They eventually came up with a so-called PVC fibre after much research. From this they prepared not only flying combinations but a whole wardrobe. As the material was white I was dressed in white trousers, shirt and socks, even my necktie and shoes were made from it. It was important that the clothing should be flame-resistant in contact with the fuel and only disintegrate. If that happened the whole suit would disintegrate leaving me naked. But it would not burn!

We made such good progress that there were days when we cancelled standing tests and I flew in the morning. With my 'ship of the desert', the He 112, we made only the basic tests necessary for the most primitive form of the motor. We worked tireless, night and day, in that year 1937! Now and again we would have a disagreement, for we were not always of the same opinion, understandable since we came from different firms and service branches though gripped by the same idea. Skill and humour got us over our differences. After completing the He 112 research using both types of rocket motor and the rocket boosters for take-offs we dismantled our marquees. At the end of 1937, a few days before Christmas, the last workshop caravan pulled out of Neuhardenberg. Meanwhile Peenemünde was under construction.

Ground testing the He 112.

CHAPTER FIVE

Peenemünde

Neuhardenberg had been only an intermediate station for carrying out the first flight tests. It was never the intention that Neuhardenberg should be the final test centre for rocket and jet turbine development as later Peenemünde became. Neuhardenberg was envisaged by RLM for a couple of months, and these months turned into a year! But how was Peenemünde chosen?

Here I have to go back a few years. In 1935, after the first development successes of von Braun's A1 and A2 rockets, the Army Weapons Office noticed that Kummersdorf would not be large enough for the new scheme and approval was given by OKH for a new testing site. The location remained to be determined. The site had to be on the coast so that von Braun could fire his later A4 rocket (the V–2) from the land to fall into the sea at the end of its trajectory. Von Braun had obtained an old Junkers Junior for his personal use since he only had the limited pilot's licence and he spent several days crabbing along the entire coastline looking for a suitable spot but without success. One day over Rügen Island he saw a nice place near the beach which from the air looked suitable for a testing station, and he touched down. Dusk fell quickly and he spent the night there after getting the local SA troop to keep watch over his aircraft. He told nobody about his plans of course. The following morning he noticed on the beach many surveyors' measuring staffs and asked the SA men the reason.

The SA leader told him proudly, "This is going to be the KdF swimming pool"! Hearing the term KdF (Strength through Joy) and the name Robert Ley, von Braun went to his aircraft immediately and took off. Before Hitler's seizure of power, Robert Ley had been a leading orator of the NSDAP, became Reich Organisations Leader and head of the German Workers' Front (DAF).

Von Braun's A4 rocket, later to become the V-2, during an early launch from Peenemünde.

Von Braun flew over Peenemünde, the most northerly point of Usedom island. He liked the look of it from the air. Spending Christmas with his parents, he told them of his aims, and mentioned

Usedom. His mother knew the region well and advised him to look at the island again, particularly the Peenemünde Haken. A few days later he viewed the Hook from the air, landed and said, "This is the very place". Von Braun reported on Peenemünde to OKH. They agreed on the site. When RLM discovered that OKH was proposing to build its own testing station for rocket research there it did not wish to be left out in the cold: *Oberstleutnant* von Richthofen, head of the RLM research division, had been following the Kummersdorf tests with great interest. In 1936 agreement was reached between OKH and RLM to consolidate the test station and expand it to

Building work underway during the expansion of Peenemünde.

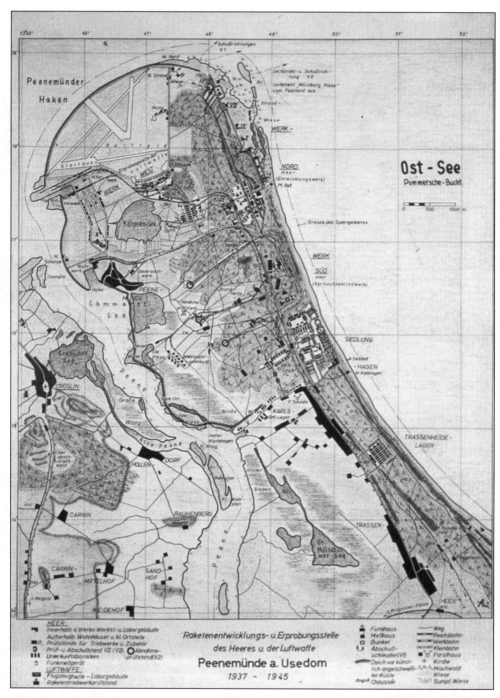

A plan of the test facility at Peenemünde.

Accommodation and relaxation buildings were part of the newly developed Peenemünde site.

Peenemünde from the air.

accommodate both. Influential personalities were interested and everything ran smoothly not least because the usual bureaucracy could be circumvented to some extent for reasons of secrecy. In 1937 while we were still running our tests at Neuhardenberg, at Peenemünde the buildings, offices and hangars were shooting up. These comprised *Werk Ost* (the Army development site) and *Werk West* (*Luftwaffe* zone with airfield). Later *Werk Nord* was added. It was intended to mass-produce the V-2 here although ultimately nothing came of this plan. Meanwhile, fantastic giant housing estates were built. Peenemünde was an imposing development for these, and

Bomb damage after the first air raid.

An aerial shot of the first major raid on Peenemünde by the RAF on 18 August 1943. A Lancaster bomber can be seen above the target at a lower level.

The entrance archway as it was in 1939 and then in 1957.

From the left, Erich, Pauls and von Braun.

also for its projects and gigantic works devoted to testing and development. The first major air raid came at last on 18 August 1943. The main weight of the attack hit the residential settlements and not the technical works. Only a section of *Werk Ost* was hit while the test stands were undamaged. We had always secretly reckoned that this attack would come, but for some incomprehensible reason it was held back for years.

At Christmas 1937 we dismantled our marquees but could

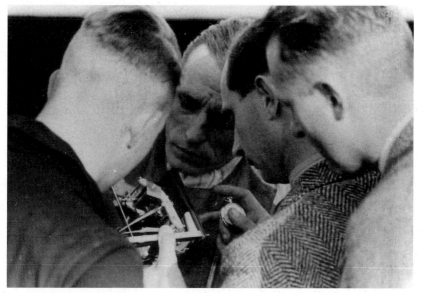

Erich, facing the camera, in deep study of a technical adjustment.

Erich, right, and from the left Cerny, Blüthner and Pauls beside a Fieseler Fi 156 Storch.

obviously not simply move to Peenemünde because the essential research installation was incomplete. Industry used the time, particularly Heinkel, to press ahead intensively. The firm of Walter and also von Braun returned to Kummersdorf while I stayed at RLM: our entire club was thus distibuted across various locations although we maintained close contact. Von Braun went to Peenemünde in February 1938, and those of us with the *Luftwaffe*, to which I was now attached, arrived on 1 April.

The He 112 at Peenemünde.

With a relatively small team of 100 men we resumed testing the Walter rocket aboard the He 112. I made a whole series of flights. The measurements division was on the ground, independent of where I flew, and I reported my data down to them to the last detail. Becoming more brazen I tried the following manouevre. Envisaging the additional thrust from the rocket as an inbuilt booster, I took off with the Junkers engine full out together

Erich flying the He 112 using the Walter rocket during take-off.

A rare overhead view of the He 112.

with the rocket running. The ascent was almost vertical! I looped the loop under rocket power alone. That also appeared fantastic! Therefore I did it a few more times, more as preparations for displays and exhibitions and so convince people of the viability of the project. One day I risked taking off using the rocket motor only with the piston engine running in neutral and the propellors disengaged.

Walter Künzel:

. . .The flights using the rocket motor to take off with the propellor feathered were much more difficult. With this kind of take-off procedure the rudder forces created by the propellor were absent. Despite the most careful placing of the rocket axis, the aircraft wandered continually. Holding direction by use of the brakes was only partially successful and wasted a lot of energy. The problem was eventually solved by the use of a jet rudder fitted at the centre of the engine jet and only effective with full rudder application. . .

We churned out take-offs with the Junkers engine cut out and the propellor idle, using 300 kg thrust, enough to lift off the He 112 into a climb and fly a half circuit. The aircraft was very light to fly and forgiving of error. I always flew around the perimeter. That took up the 30 seconds burn time leaving me nicely placed to glide down to the landing strip. Apart from a few minor defects there was never a problem with the Walter rocket. It never cut out again and worked excellently in every respect.

Walter Künzel:

. . . At that time there was a clear application in military technology for our pioneering research work. In 1936 and 1937 no thought was being given to light jet motors with powerful thrust, although the demand existed for a fighter with a fast rate of climb. A rocket motor supplementary to the piston engine in a standard fighter would assist the climb and so solve the problem. A comprehensive programme of flights carried out first at Neuhardenberg and later on the airfield at Peenemünde with the He 112 resulted in this requirement being solved in the form we had envisaged. . .

Thus came into being the He 176. . .

CHAPTER SIX

Heinkel He 176 – The Project

The allegation often repeated by technical experts that Heinkel made the first rocket aircraft, the He 176, as a 'black machine', without the approval of, or having been contracted by, the RLM, is totally false. The RLM was always fully in the picture about the He 176 and Heinkel's intentions – and was involved! In 1936 RLM awarded Heinkel a contract to build the world's first pure rocket aircraft.

Walter Künzel:

> . . .The He 176 project came into existence during the flight trials of the He 112 at Neuhardenberg. It was a bold project for the time and involved numerous new problems. At this time the term 'interceptor' was being bandied about and the He 176 was to be the research aircraft for the 'interceptor'. . .

RLM was therefore proposing to have designed for the *Luftwaffe* a new type of aircraft. By virtue of its enormous rate of climb it would take off almost vertically when an enemy bomber formation came into sight at 6000 to 7000 metres, head for it at full speed, make a banking attack from below at high speed while firing from its machine-guns or cannons, and once the tanks were dry land again.

The record-breaking flight of the Messerschmitt Me 163A-V4 on 2 October 1941. This type became operational in May, 1944, known as the Komet.

From the left: Speer, Milch, Dittmar and Kröger.

The German hierarchy viewing early flights made by the Me 163.

An Me 163B-V2 as a glider in 1942.

An Me 163A takes off and climbs almost vertically.

The Me 163, which was developed and tested independently of the He 176, came later, during the Second World War, as an operational interceptor.

On the agenda for discussion was: 'What should we build and how should we build it on the basis of our experiences to date?' There were two possibilities:

(i) the 'rocket-only aircraft' with a certain safety margin won naturally at the cost of performance or

(ii) a smaller aircraft with a greater risk factor which would eventually have a speed in excess of 1000 kms/hr. After extensive discussions chaired by Dr Heinkel he said: "Really it is Warsitz who must decide, since in the end he is the man who has to fly it. What is your opinion, what do you favour?" Before the entire syndicate I replied, "Herr Doktor, I am for the latter proposal!"

Deployment of an Me 163 in Bad Zwischenahn.

When Heinkel and I went over the concept on several occasions subsequently, we were both agreed – secretly – that we were aiming to break the world speed record with the first rocket aircraft, and with 'three zeros', that is, at least 1000 kms/hr! I should like to emphasize once more how important Heinkel was for the entire development. God knows he had a millstone round his neck, and so could not attend to every minor detail which happened to crop up. The possible novelties interested him, but the He 176 became his manic obsession in every respect! We were also glad at his interest in the He 176 for everything went that much smoother when he had the say. This enthusiasm went hand in glove with pressure, of course – nothing was ever being done fast enough. He was in the picture about every detail and attended to minor particulars personally. Despite that the cooperation was extremely enjoyable, for I worked intensively with Hertel and Heinkel. Both were men prepared to take a risk and did not count the pennies when it came to a new project. Occasionally they had to take account of reverses, and these we certainly had in sufficient numbers.

Since the development of the He 176 was subject to the greatest secrecy, Heinkel set up a special department at his Rostock-Marienehe works. The initial standing trials were to be run in a wooden barrack hut to which very few works employees had access. From this 'booth of boarding' a permanent building was soon in place, in record time for Heinkel. The various offices for the 'special development' were upstairs. The research progressed rapidly and in parallel with the construction of the mock rig. After completion of the first one we were amazed at how tiny it was. A thing like that! I think we were all convinced it would never fly!

Walter Künzel:

> . . . In building the mock-up we sat Herr Warsitz on a parachute and tailored everything around him. The greatest diameter of the fuselage was only 700 mm. The He 176 could well claim to have the smallest cockpit in which anybody ever flew. . .

The He 176 was so small that it could have fitted into a room at the social centre. The overall surface area including the fuselage was five square metres. Wingspan was 5 metres, fuselage length 5.5 metres, height with undercarriage down 1.44 metres, wheelbase 700 mm. Wheels up the airplane was relatively low, the height of a writing desk, about one metre – and a grown man was to fit inside it?

After numerous surveys and modifications, mainly to the cockpit arrangement, influenced exclusively by myself, construction of the so called V1 prototype was begun at above-average tempo. (V1 = *Versuchsmuster* 1, Heinkel He 176-V1, the first prototype, and nothing to do with the V-1 flying bomb!)

CHAPTER SEVEN

He 176 – Construction and Development

The first sketches were drawn in 1937 during our Neuhardenberg sojourn, and a lot of water flowed under the bridge before the maiden flight in 1939!

The He 176 was an aircraft of a new era, just subsonic, and so a new design in which a host of difficulties presented themselves to be overcome. Completely new was the wingflow profile designed for supersonic speed whose leading edges were razor sharp. This increased the danger of losing the airstream at lower speeds needed for safe landings. It was naturally rather difficult, however, to design a high performance aircraft with the flight characteristics of a Ju 52 – the old 'Aunt Ju' who virtually put herself down! The wings had been designed from the beginning as fuel containers but the riveting was problematical because the wings were so flat and only explosive studs were suitable. Luckily we did have some experience otherwise we would never have got the wings leakproof.

Walter Künzel:

> . . . The wing was elliptical, the profile symmetrical with a rear sweep of 40% and a thickness of 9%. For calculation purposes at that time almost no data was available. The only useful file was NACA 492 (Stark & Dönhoff). This report dealt with profile measurements for propellors and the deductions permissible were Ca and Cw values. Nothing was available regarding stability. The fuel containers were real works of art in welding technology and with the new Arcatom-welding process for light metals this was true pioneering in the craft. If you consider that the greatest thickness of the wing was 90 mm and we had to weld

the wing leakproof for 82% H_2O_2 (hydrogen peroxide) you can form a picture of the great difficulty which had to be overcome.

The arrangement of the cockpit caused a problem solved by having the pilot semi-recumbent. In a steep climb I was to some extent hanging head down. A very uncomfortable situation!

Walter Künzel:

> The semi-recumbent pilot's position was not only chosen to avoid resistance and to save space and weight, but primarily so that the pilot could better tolerate the expected high acceleration.

The cockpit was so narrow that I could touch the sides with a hand but not bend the elbow, and so my space available was very restricted. This meant that levers operated by a particular hand had to be installed on the opposite side. This forced me to lean the hand across my body and change hands on the control stick. It was as if I were seated in a made-to-measure shoe! Later in flight it would often happen that when entering the cockpit I would forget my wallet in my rear pocket. Once seated it restricted my movements and was very uncomfortable. I would then have to shift about to wrestle it free and hand it to my ground crew for safe keeping, so narrow was the cockpit!

Walter Künzel:

> Very great efforts were also made to provide a cockpit with a full panorama, balancing good visibility optics with the necessary strength.

The cockpit, including the forward bubble – therefore the entire nose – was made of plexiglass which had to be free of any distortion. After massive development work this problem was resolved by the Hamburg firm Kopperschmidt. The roof was also plexiglass.

Walter Künzel:

> In an emergency at lower speeds the cockpit cover could be thrown free by the pilot allowing him to make the normal exit by parachute.

As I would be flying this aircraft for the first time at speeds never previously obtained, baling out in the familiar way would have meant certain death. One could not have left the aircraft in the conventional manner because at the higher speeds it would not have been possible to get clear of the aircraft. If I had stuck my head out it would certainly have been torn off!

Safety was the major worry but new inventions frequently call upon us to reject safety in pursuit of the goal: this was naturally the case with breathtaking speed and unorthodox flying machines such as the first rocket and jet aircraft. In the case of the Heinkel He 178 jet, which I will describe later, I sat on a standard parachute in an area which would not have reached 1000 kms/hr. The rocket would have! In consequence, Heinkel for his part did everything he could to ensure my safety. Because of the poor chance of getting free of it, the whole cockpit had to be made ejectable. The cockpit and bulkhead behind me were fixed to four locks and were not integral to the fuselage. Between them – in layman's terms – were powder cartridges ignited by moving a lever to release the locks and so free the cockpit. The tests were time consuming because we couldn't get the powder right. Eventually we used 200 atm. compressed air to do the trick.

Walter Künzel:

Once the work to build the machine was well advanced, a model was tested in Dr Tietgenz' DVL high speed wind tunnel. Tests were in windspeeds of up to 0.9 Mach. The model was of steel and 180 mm long, probably the first such model to be tested for such high speeds. The need to achieve accuracy, particularly in the wings and tailplane, caused us a great deal of concern because there were no workshops for high speed models. The cockpit testing had already been done very carefully on the ground. The closing off and separation from the fuselage was studied from every conceivable situation using different angles and long elasticated ropes. We made hundreds of catapult launches in the secret hangar for the Marienehe 'special development' and also later at Peenemünde.

In order to determine the effect of a landing for a pilot trapped in the detached cockpit with his own parachute, Dr (med) Ruff prepared a dummy. It was manufactured in such a way that conclusions could be drawn as to the type of injuries a pilot might receive. The effect of forces caused by the seat straps when the cockpit hit the ground were also measured and conclusions drawn as to possible internal injuries, etc.

A Berlin firm which manufactured artificial limbs made the dummy – 'Warsitz' – to my measurements and weight distribution, and the tests were run in parallel with the building of the aircraft. 'Warsitz' was strapped into a wooden cockpit slung below an He 111. We then climbed to altitude and released the cockpit. The braking parachute then deployed automatically at 100 kms/hr. We wanted to establish if a pilot – in this case myself – could withstand the fast twisting of the cockpit after detachment from the fuselage, or would fall unconscious.

Everything was charted, the results showing that generally though luck was needed, normally a person would be able to withstand the rapid acceleration and braking movements of the parachute.

Walter Künzel:

It transpired from these tests that if the pilot landed on quite soft ground, serious injuries were not to be expected.

For reasons of secrecy all tests were made at Peenemünde, the cockpit often falling into the sea and being retrieved each time from the bottom by a motor launch putting out from Greifswalder Bodden, secured to the stern of the boat and towed ashore. It was not a comforting sight to see the cockpit porpoising along with its airman occupant – the wooden 'Warsitz' – behind the launch. In such moments I would think to myself, 'If that is how you are going to be fished out, you won't be grinning like you are now!'

The theory was that in order to eject free at 1000 kms/hr and get down safely I would have to reach 6000 metres altitude and operate the following procedure: With my right hand pull a lever on the bulkhead behind me, just to the left of the back of my head, to separate the cockpit from the fuselage. The cockpit would then be fired free to fall below. The open area vacated by the cockpit would cause the aircraft to become sluggish, and break apart in due course,

Erich relaxes aboard one of the retreival motor launches during the experiments to evaluate the pilot ejection system of the He 176.

Two of the retreival boats operating from Peenemünde.

a fact which would not much interest the pilot as his cockpit descended. The cockpit would turn over three or four times before it began to oscillate. Behind the cockpit a braking parachute was installed, this could not be deployed until the speed of descent decreased to avoid parting the lines. After I had fallen about 1000 metres the wind resistance would slow the cockpit. With my left hand I would now pull another lever behind my back to deploy the braking parachute. This would restrain the vertical descent of the cockpit relatively quickly to a final speed of 300 kms/hr. This was too fast a speed for the pilot to expect to survive. He would then throw off the plexiglass cover, unbuckle his straps, jump out, fall to 800 to 1000 metres and deploy the personal parachute to reach the ground at a speed of about 4 to 5 metres/sec.

Walter Künzel:

> For various reasons the fuselage of the completed machine had to be lengthened by 120 mm forward at the beginning of 1939. We extended the cockpit forward and were able to install a much larger cockpit parachute so that the descent velocity of cockpit and pilot was reduced to 15 metres/sec.

I was quite prepared to go through with this manouevre but it was never tried in practice. It is a most unpleasant sensation for a pilot to be forced to abandon his aircraft. All results and test data are lost and the work had served no purpose. Comfort in the knowledge that one can get to safety allows latitude for experiment, however: 'Now let the thing blow up if need be, you have your parachute and simply jump overboard!' We therefore had an ejector-cockpit, the forerunner of the modern ejector seat, obviously quite different technically, but serving the same purpose.

The first rocket engine, for safety reasons the Walter engine, built into the He 176 had 600 kgs thrust. Combustion was the 'cold Walter process'.

Walter Künzel:

> It was found that the fuel had to be pumped, and not forced through by pressure as had been done with the He 112. The Walter works solved this problem quickly and satisfactorily.

In some steep climbs with the He 112 I had noticed that the standard instrumentation did not register correctly. Accurate instruments are rather important for a pilot! It was not so much the speed as the vertical flight. As a consequence, firms of instrument makers were contacted and asked to develop as soon as possible the instruments we needed for vertical ascents.

Where to place the large levers and the engine was a difficult question. The RLM had made a number of unreasonable demands which had had to be taken into consideration during the building of the He 176, and this first prototype had two shafts for two machine-guns right and left of the pilot, therefore between the pilot seat and outer shell, just at the very spot where the instrument panel was wanted! There were subsequently several conferences at RLM in which considerable friction was generated, for Heinkel himself, his men and I insisted that it was madness to start planning where to put machine guns in a pure unflown new design such as the rocket-aircraft was, and about which nothing was known regarding its behaviour either at low or high speed. Since the RLM was not to be moved, we had no choice but to fit the shafts because the gentlemen often came on inspection visits. We explained that the shafts were being used temporarily to house the instruments, rods and so on.

There was no proper instrument panel as such, for even the smallest one would have seriously hampered my vision from the semi-recumbent position. The control surfaces were operated as normal: the rudder by foot pedal, ailerons and elevator from the control stick. The stick was very short since no force was needed at the higher speeds, the merest finger pressure had a vast effect.

Walter Künzel:

The gaps between cockpit and fuselage were responsible for a certain weakness in the frame which could have unpleasant effects at high speeds. Equally unpleasant were the control stick movements caused by forces at high speeds: the forces acting on the control surfaces were very great and the movement of the stick very small so that the pilot lost the necessary feel. We solved the problem by putting the attack point for the steering rods on a spindle-nut which transferred to a spindle on the underside of the control column. By turning the head of the control stick the pilot could adapt the rudder movements and steering forces to the conditions. The first flight tests were made in the wind tunnel. We hung the original aircraft in the large wind tunnel at the Göttingen Test Institute and made the calculations for the take-off and landing conditions. At the same time Herr Warsitz had the opportunity to familiarize himself with the steering pressures and variability of the rudder deflections.

Once the hull finally had its instrumentation and motor installed, Udet gave permission for testing at Peenemünde. Because of the need for secrecy and the smallness of Heinkel's airfield at Rostock-Marienehe it would not have been possible there. The He 176 was to be transferred under military escort to Peenemünde one night in June 1938. A ticklish situation arose for me beforehand when Udet and General-Ingenieur Lucht arrived at Peenemünde with the RLM Staff on another matter.

Lucht took me aside and said, "Herr Warsitz, you are not flying the He 176." This took away my breath for a moment. "Herr Lucht, why ever not?" I retorted.

"Because you are the only person who has made rocket-powered flights in the other machines and we view the He 176 as risky. We cannot allow you to gamble with your life!"

I was mollified to know that the ban was in my best interests of survival, but replied nevertheless, "Herr Lucht, I do not agree and I should like to inform General Udet of that immediately!"

"OK," he said, "I shan't take it the wrong way, do as you see fit."

I went over to the assembled crowd of officers and complained to Udet, "Herr Generaloberst, General-Ingenieur Lucht has informed me that I am not to fly the He 176!"

"And why not?" he wanted to know.

"Perhaps Herr Lucht can give a better explanation than I, I have only just been informed."

Lucht butted in,

"Herr Generaloberst, it is for the safety reasons we discussed previously, and moreover it is a Heinkel aircraft! Heinkel built it and is carrying out the full test programme, and he should use his own pilots for that. The RLM does not want to gamble the life of our Warsitz!"

"Herr Generaloberst," I countered, "that appears to be a mistaken point of view! Quite apart from the fact that I definitely want to be the first pilot to fly the machine, for I have done the necessary preliminary work, I am convinced that all will go well if I fly her because I know her not only the hull from the first coat of paint, but also the rocket engine. Furthermore, she actually was made to measure for me, from the cockpit to the operating levers!"

Udet responded:

"Well, that can easily be changed! But gentlemen, I have to agree with Warsitz. He has risked his arse to this point and now when it comes to the crunch, when the time has come to earn his laurels, you want somebody else to have all the glory. In any case,

From the right: Künzel, Erich and General Jeschonek in deep discussion.

I am convinced that the maiden flight will only go well if Warsitz flies the aircraft, and because he knows her. I am in favour of letting him risk his neck – he will be successful!"

I beamed and thanked – with that it was decided.

The He 176 arrived safely at Peenemünde. Künzel had been with the machine every second of the journey. She was rolled into Hangar W1. There under the supervision of Walter Künzel and myself, and with the assistance of the many engineers, assemblers and technical people from Heinkel she was readied and the wings remounted. The joy on the faces of all the Heinkel ground crew was astonishing to see. Nothing else could be expected of ourselves obviously, but the assembly workers had put themselves into it body and soul to such an extent that I might almost say they were 'obsessed', regardless of what it took they were available day and night and it happened more than once that we worked 36 or 48 hours at a stretch without an hour's sleep. Now and again at night one saw an assembly worker almost keel over, and then he would be dragged away to a corner of the hangar or to our special dormitory for an hour's sleep even though he fought against it.

From the right: Pauls, Erich and von Braun relax over a glass of wine.

Heinkel was in charge of the test programme and not Peenemünde. The latter made available the airfield with all necessary equipment and installations but was to be not involved in any way with the testing nor to influence affairs. At my express wish, Heinkel had reserved this right for himself at RLM, whereby a certain tension arose between Heinkel and Peenemünde, because Peenemünde people of the *Luftwaffe* division, who God knows were not up to scratch technically, attempted to meddle. Often they hid themselves behind the skirts of RLM to wheedle themselves into the trials, which was unpleasant! Only a small Peenemünde nucleus, people actually required for the general work, were involved in it. All other work was done by Heinkel staff.

Von Braun's cooperation with ourselves and Heinkel could not be better because he was a very decent chap. Although not technically part of the He 176-V1 project with the Walter rocket engine, naturally everything affecting it was of interest to himself and his colleagues because the He 176-V2 was to have the von Braun engine, and he collated all data we made in standing tests, rolling tests and later flights for evaluation purposes.

We began again with standing testing. The engine had a more powerful 600 kg thrust and we experienced many setbacks. Modifications would ensue followed by more tests. We worked literally day and night! After we had got the engine to the stage where we could forecast: 'It is ready for the maiden flight', the time had come for the rolling tests.

CHAPTER EIGHT

Heinkel He 176 – Leaps into the Air

Obviously one cannot simply just get into a unique new aircraft and take off. Initially the basic, unknown characteristics on the ground have to be ascertained first. We began very cautiously and expected more difficulties during tests under tow by the heaviest and fastest road vehicles we could find. From the Mercedes office in Berlin we found a 7.6 litre compressor vehicle for charter, and bought it. Other military offices would have had to submit the usual request which no doubt would have been rejected eventually by the accounting office with the terse observation 'too expensive'. Naturally there would follow hours of haggling and memoranda as long as your arm, all of which took up time. We dispensed with all that! We took the decision ourselves, telephoned it through next day and our vehicles sergeant would go to the vendor and fetch the purchase.

When the compressor vehicle arrived I got in straight away and we set off. On the short concrete access road to the airfield it did 120 kms/hr. Once I got on the field – but without the aircraft in tow – I never exceeded 140 kms/hr because the soft grass offered tremendous resistance. When we made the first rolling tests with the aircraft somebody else drove the vehicle while I rode in the aircraft cockpit. Top speed was 100 kms/hr, nothing like fast enough to test the rudder, which on the He 176 was very small and made especially for very high speeds.

At 110 kms/hr no matter how I worked the control stick it had no effect on the aircraft. One thing we did establish was that the 700 mm wheelbase turned the rolling test into a crazy affair: the least unevenness of the ground while under tow and a wing would touch the ground, tearing off a wingcap or causing a ground-spin.

'This is no use!' I exclaimed, 'it doesn't prove anything! We must have higher speeds. The Mercedes can do 165, where best to try it?' At that moment the idea struck me that I should run the tests on the beach. Usedom island had a fantastic sandy shore stretching from the northern tip at Peenemünde to Swinemünde town 15 kilometres away. That it curved was irrelevant. I drove the Mercedes – without the aircraft – to the beach and drove full out all the way to Swinemünde. I reached 155 kms/hr along the hard sand right at the shore's edge. I was pleased at the speed because the friction from the sand was nowhere near so great as with the airfield grass. Just short of Swinemünde when I tried to reverse the wheels stuck fast for a moment and I sank down. I rang for a tractor to pull me out. This also sank in the sand. A towing vehicle came out from the airfield. Anchored to a large tree it winched us free. The whole thing was another useless escapade, for it proved impossible to tow an aircraft on sand. The ground runs had to be done under the aircraft's own power.

These rolling tests began at the end of 1938. I got used to how the He 176 would shoot forward, but at the same moment I had to throttle back, for on the first test the left wing touched the ground for an unlevel surface and I span. No damage was caused but it was a regular occurrence. Since after each run we did not want to be fitting new wing caps, which took half a day to make, we fitted a metal shoe below the wingtip. When the wing inevitably touched the ground, the metal shoe slipped along and prevent the wing cap being broken off. A small fleet of vehicles inspected the rolling strip before tests, and later before take-offs to see whether moles were at work in the area, even the smallest molehill was enough to cause disaster. A crash had to be avoided under all circumstances, any misfortune might have been enough for the whole project to be cancelled. We had to proceed with great caution, as Dr Heinkel always hammered into me, a demand easier to make than do when testing an entirely new kind of aircraft.

In a conventional aircraft, at the moment when one goes to full power one immediately has the ability to steer, that is to say the rudder at the rear needed to keep the heading for take-off has immediate effect due to the airstream from the propellors. Our great difficulty was that the He 176 had no propellor and thus created no wind for the rudder. The rudder only began to take effect during a ground run when one reached take-off speed, and before this had no effect at all. To correct that, on the take-off strip I had to hold the heading by use of the brakes, left or right. This was a very sensitive and dangerous affair, for if a little too much pressure was applied on one side the aircraft would either enter into a spin or the tail would go up and threaten to somersault the machine. Though it happened a few times, we always got away with it. Occasionally the machine looked as if it would flip over, but it never did so completely.

Walter Künzel:

'As it was almost impossible to achieve take-off using brakes alone, because there was no airstream for the rudder, to keep the aircraft in the required direction and save energy we introduced a jet rudder, which was only effective with full rudder movements.'

Towards the end of 1938 some structural changes to the hull and engine were necessary. We dedicated the winter months to the task and in the spring of 1939 went ahead with the preliminary tests. I had advanced the rolling tests so far that I would roar the machine full out from the airfield boundary until she lifted off. A kind of leap into the air would ensue, then I would shut down the engine and land again. These flights did not look too good from the ground! At take-off the aircraft would wobble, yaw left and right and back again and then fall. All at two metres altitude, later five! As the leaps got bigger I could see that the airfield was not long enough. It had to be extended very urgently to provide a take-off strip towards the west between 800 and 1000 metres long, while on the other side the woods had to be cut down to give me a better chance of stopping, or for a better airstrip. Later concrete airstrips were laid at Peenemünde. We started building the airfield in 1937, before then there had only been sea, marsh, moor and woods here.

I flew a whole series of short 'flights' – over one hundred – under the aircraft's own power up to 10 to 20 metres altitude: these were only short leaps estimated at over 100 metres long. Up to this time we had deliberately kept the *Luftwaffe* generals in the dark but in the end could not prevent an RLM visit headed by Udet, Milch and half the General Staff. When they arrived in May 1939, the He 176 was already on the airfield in front of the hangar.

After his examination Udet said laconically: "Man, you call those wings? They're running boards!" Then he turned to me: "And you want to fly it?"

"Why not," I replied, "she has already flown, if only short flights, but she has been in the air!"

Some of the most senior officers stayed on the field while the others retreated to the boundary. Then I demonstrated the short flight. Unfortunately the wind did not play along so that I had to use an uneven strip to take off. This made the run, the brief waggle in the air, the whole flight and landing – I was close to overshooting and had to intentionally spin to a standstill – look like a disaster! After getting out I was driven to where the generals and Dr Heinkel were waiting. Milch was the first to approach. He congratulated me and promoted me on the spot to *Flugkapitän* for my special achievement. Udet and everybody else who had seen it also offered their congratulations.

The short demonstration flight of the He 176 for Milch and Udet.

Milch and Udet plus entourage during their visit to view progress of the He 176.

Discussion as to the future of the He 176.

Next there was a heated discussion and as a result the He 176 was grounded. Udet was behind the ban. "How can anyone build such a thing?" he asked. He knew previously about the He 176 – perhaps not the precise details, not how small it was. "This is not an aircraft you have built here. Why didn't you build a larger machine for the new engine and aim for more safety?"

At that I became involved. I got on well with Udet and knew I might risk making a comment: "Herr *Generaloberst*, it is my fault. I was and am convinced that these flights, which are necessary, will go off smoothly with the 176. I know her down to the minutest detail ever since the first stroke of the pencil at the drawing board!" He would not back down, and the ban remained in force. "Every good landing is a failed crash," he told me in parting.

The *Luftwaffe* gentlemen had a look round at everything else, and after they had gone, Dr Heinkel, Künzel and I sat on a boarding ladder to discuss the proceedings. "So what do we do now?" I said to Dr Heinkel, "I really think you might have objected, that would have been the right thing to do."

"I know Udet and Milch," Heinkel replied, "it was not the right time. I would like to make that clear!"

Without Heinkel's knowledge I flew to Berlin and begged Udet to allow us to proceed with the flight programme. I promised by all that was holy to be careful, and I gave him my personal guarantee, although I could hardly guarantee that nothing would happen, of course. I appealed to his conscience. "Success depends on these flights which are necessary and the way forward into a whole new direction for aviation." I had judged his mood right. He dismissed me with the words, "Go and do as you please, but take care!" I thanked him and returned to Peenemünde with the words, "We carry on, Udet has approved it!" I carried out a host of short 'flights', and after more modifications to the hull we gradually approached the point when we could consider the first real flight.

CHAPTER NINE

Heinkel He 176 – The Maiden Flight

Heinkel's wish to witness the first flight was shared by Udet and many at RLM. I was basically opposed, for generally when one shows off a new aircraft for the first time before so many people something is bound to go wrong. Impartiality is then lost and the observers become impatient. In consequence Künzel, Bartelsen and I – despite our assurances to Udet and Heinkel – were agreed that the maiden flight should be held in secret.

This important day in the history of aviation was now at hand. Nobody from RLM, nor Herr Walter, nor our own Dr Heinkel, nor any of the Peenemünde heads, nor anybody from the *Luftwaffe* or Army was invited. Film cameramen, the boys who did the measuring and anybody else directly involved obviously had to come, but nothing official. Once the running tests had accustomed me to the aircraft's peculiarities and perfidious little tricks at ever greater speeds, on the late evening of a fine early day of summer I made the decision to go ahead with the maiden flight after making five 'leaps' without problems. If these few short flights went well, I had told myself beforehand, tomorrow I shall make the first circuit and then head for the skies.

In my time as an aviator, whenever planning something uncertain, I would always cast aside any irrelevancies. But on that evening of 19 June 1939 in my bachelor home – I had a nice little house at Peenemünde – I put my affairs in order. It was the first time I had done such a thing, and I asked myself, is it going to be OK tomorrow? As the mood of the pilot for such maiden flights is decisive, and on 20 June 1939 I was in very good physical shape, I told Künzel, "The next flight is a circuit!" This meant it would be the first proper flight in history by a manned rocket aircraft. Künzel nodded, only Asmund Bartelsen wanted a postponement for the 21st because he wanted to check over the engine thoroughly before I attempted the circuit.

"Listen, Bartelsen," I told him, "on five hops your engine held out and it will do so on the sixth. Don't change anything or overhaul it. Just have the engine ready for the first flight." After my decision to fly immediately all the engineers and ground crew went very quiet, nobody spoke a word, all knew that the decisive moment for the future was at hand. I packed my parachute myself – purely occupation therapy – something I always did to calm myself when I faced a dangerous time. I took Künzel aside and asked him to forward a letter in my drawer in the event of my death. It was also my custom to take my leave very heartily of my most faithful companion, my dog, whenever I knew that a perilous flight or standing test confronted me.

The machine was made ready at a feverish rate. Künzel and his people checked the aircraft over while I undressed. I took some sun and prepared myself mentally for take-off. I closed my eyes and tried to relax, although I heard the others in the background working on the aircraft. I thought of Heinkel, Udet and all those who wanted to be present, of my people at home, from whom I had heard only once: immersed in my thoughts I was alone with myself – total stillness – and mentally I went over all the procedures with the tiny He 176 once again – every movement, from switching on the motor to the take-off. But then what? How would she behave in the air at full throttle? My train of thought was broken by some happy laughter and loud squealing: some of the ground staff had fetched a porker from a yard forming part of the adjacent farm at the airfield boundary. This was to be my good-luck charm!

There is only one photo of me, holding the piglet. Unfortunately the 176 is not in it, it was only three metres away. Perhaps it was for the best: if the machine had been included, I might not have got the print. To the best of my knowledge there are neither sketches nor original prints of the He 176 extant today. After the war all efforts of Professor Heinkel, Wernher von Braun and myself to obtain one failed despite our contacts. We knew that films and photographs had been taken at Peenemünde, for every day at every standing test and

Erich with his lucky charm piglet.

test flight at least three film cameramen were present. When I informed Udet then that I would like to have some of the photos as a souvenir he replied: "Warsitz, you can all have as many as you want, and copies of the films too, but only when the 'plane comes off the secret list!" The result is that in my private collection today I do not have a single photograph because all documentation and film material were captured by the Soviets at the capitulation and are no longer accessible to us. If I had anticipated the historical importance I would have taken a few photos on the sly, but from pure honesty and lack of time we never thought of doing it.

I dressed in my flying combinations and went to the machine. Meanwhile the film cameramen had got wind of the planned flight and were naturally anxious to hold things up until they were ready. An unpleasant feeling! I always hated it when before such flights the Leica people or the camera operators were hanging around because they always gave me an impression of wanting to 'hold you up until the last possible moment' but for technical reasons it was unavoidable.

During the preparations for a maiden flight one is naturally a little unsettled, nothing is being done quickly enough, but once in the cockpit I was tranquillity itself. I strapped myself in and checked over all the levers while the rocket people worked aft. The wingtanks were topped up, but for weight reasons not to the maximum – we increased that later. The hull and control surfaces were checked one more time, everybody was swarming around the aircraft, and then came the command, 'Ready for take-off!' I got the signal that the airstrip was clear. Künzel came over and shook my hand without speaking, tears in his eyes – we were really quite close friends. Well, it was not my way to get all soft and so I looked away because God knows I needed to concentrate on other things. The ground crew closed the canopy and pushed the machine the few metres to the airstrip and opened the slats in the fuselage. 'Ready for take-off!' the command rapped out again. I put the tanks under pressure, the pressure rose to optimum, I opened the throttle full, the rocket roared full out and the machine hissed forward.

I was already familiar with the unusual acceleration on the ground. I required a longer airstrip with the almost full fuel tanks. I held the machine on course using the lightest touch on one or other brake and at 300 kms/hr, shortly before lifting off, she veered left. The left wing touched the ground – and I saw disaster waiting to happen. Although the airfield had been checked beforehand by two VW Kübelwagen, two men on the running boards checking for obstructions or new molehills: obviously between the check and the approach run a new molehill had appeared, and my right wheel hit it. To avoid a spin and to head the aircraft in the right direction I touched the right brake: the aircraft felt as thought it would overturn – it looked bad – and nobody would have given a *pfennig* for my chances had that happened!

I wanted this flight behind me at all costs. I gave more gas and straightened her up. On quite another heading from that originally intended she leapt into the air and flew with a yaw and a wobble. In flying, 'speed up is half the problem solved!' I kept her close to the ground while gaining speed, then pulled back gently on the control stick for a rapid ascent. I was at 750 kms/hr and without any loss in speed the machine shot skywards at an angle somewhere between vertical and 45°. She was enormously sensitive to the controls: the slightest movement of the control stick for the ailerons and she almost rolled, a millimetre of elevator and she would climb vertically or go upside down. Her speed, whether horizontal or ascending changed momentarily because of the loss of weight through the high fuel consumption. I was not too interested in fast speeds or reaching a great altitude on this first flight for lack of time, the fuel would last at most one minute. So as not to drift too far away from the airfield I banked left and, though throttled back, found myself over the Baltic. This was the last place I wanted to come down without a lifejacket – there was no room for one and I had been told that: 'If you fall in fully dressed, not being much of a swimmer, you will sink like a stone!'

Everything turned out wonderfully, however, and it was a relief to fly round the northern tip of Usedom island without a sound at 800 kms/hr. There was no time to experiment, now I had to concentrate of the landing. I banked sharp left again to straighten up for the airstrip, losing such speed and altitude as I could, and during this steep turn the rocket died as the tanks dried up. The abrupt loss of speed hurled me foward in my restraint straps. I pressed the stick forward, hissed rapidly over the Peene and came in at 500 kms/hr. I crossed the airfield boundary and after several prescribed little bounces the machine came to a stop. The world's first manned rocket flight had succeeded!

Immediately all the cars came racing up, of course. I threw back the canopy, climbed out and was chaired away on the shoulders of the ground crew. One had brought along a bottle of champagne and poured me and my closest colleagues a full glass each. We emptied them to toast the flight and in accordance with custom smashed the glasses against the aircraft's undercarriage. The jubilation and joy were great, and the revelry in the officers' mess afterwards defies description, so long had we awaited the moment.

Walter Künzel:

> None of those involved will ever forget the great impression which this maiden flight made on us all. As regards myself personally, who had overall responsibility for the preparation, and gave permission for the take-off, I may say that though outwardly calm, after the successful landing I was absolutely bathed in sweat, and several of us, myself included, had tears in our eyes once the aircraft came to a stop on the ground.

The first thing we did was briefly discuss the technical points there and then, which everybody was keen to know, and after that I told Künzel: "Now we must inform Dr Heinkel quickly!" I spoke to Heinkel and made the announcement myself: "Herr Doktor Heinkel, I must respectfully report the world's first manned rocket flight with your He 176. To prove that I survived it you have the evidence of my voice!"

"What?" was his only answer.

I replied: "Yes, now don't get mad, everything went perfectly, and we really had no opportunity to inform you or await your arrival from Rostock."

Walter Künzel:

> Unfortunately after this maiden flight, systematic development work was no longer possible. Despite all the secrecy the sensational news went round the higher circles at RLM like

Werner von Braun, holding his white hat, after he first saw Erich fly the He 176.

From the left: Pauls, Speer and Dornberger.

wildfire, and after that we basically did nothing but give demonstration flights.

Next day Dr Heinkel, Udet and a whole Staff of Peenemünde officers came to witness the second successful flight. I had my confidence up this second time and made an impressive pass at low level. When Heinkel and I were alone he told me bitterly, "Warsitz, that I missed being there for the maiden flight, I have not forgiven you for that."

CHAPTER TEN

The Demonstration for Hitler

After the first flights of the He 176 there came a call from Udet's adjutant *Oberst* Pendele to inform me that with immediate effect all future flights, including short leaps, were forbidden on the orders of the *Generaloberst*. I asked at once for the reason. "Herr *Oberst*, are the results we have achieved in recent weeks not sufficient proof? And that all flights have gone off smoothly? Who is now blocking our progress, and for what reason?"

"Warsitz, calm down," Pendele told me nicely, "There is no cause for you to get excited. There is a good reason – and you will fly it again."

Next day I learned from Heinkel that a display had been arranged for the Führer. The big air show for Hitler, the Party high-ups and the *Luftwaffe* Generals was to be at Rechlin. We were close to the outbreak of war then and Hitler was bound to have been keen to know what new ideas we were working on. The display by the 176 was to be included with the show of the newest types at the Rechlin tests centre, but not at Rechlin itself for secrecy reasons. Roggentin airfield was the chosen location. Heinkel also told me that Udet had expressly forbidden him again to carry out any work on the aircraft which might prevent its being flown at the air show. As required after each flight we had naturally made changes and modifications to the 176, but this ban meant that not only could we not fly it, we could not taxi either! From the flier's point of view we had been put on ice!

I appealed to Udet and Heinkel for the decision to be reversed using the argument that the aircraft had not yet reached its 100% level of performance. "That doesn't matter," Udet said, "the main thing is that it flies. That is a 100% success in which speed and suchlike play no part." As a test pilot and chief pilot at Peenemünde I had to obey. Very much depended on the display to the Führer. After a few days we got the date: 3 July 1939.

Once the preparations were started I flew to Rechlin with Künzel. Roggentin was about three kilometres further on. The field there was in a very good, even condition, no concrete runway, but grassy like Peenemünde – and with no buildings. After I reported myself clear to fly, I hoped only that we would have a good wind allowing us to use as much of the field as possible. We asked Rechlin for a marquee. A few days before the display a small group of us travelled at night with the hull – the wings had been removed for transport – to Roggentin and began to prepare the aircraft.

Erich arrives at Rechlin for the display flight for Hitler.

3 July 1939 dawned. The Führer arrived at Rechlin at first light. At the same time, despite the ban, I drove the aircraft across the field to test rudder, brakes and so forth. It so happened that Udet was flying into Rechlin from Berlin in his red Siebel and saw the streams of

smoke trailing the He 176. As soon as he landed he rang me: "Warsitz, come immediately to Rechlin!" It took only a few minutes to get there by car, and as soon as I entered the office, without bidding me good morning, he accused me: "You had a flight."

"Herr *Generaloberst* is mistaken."

"I saw your smoke trail from the air."

"Herr *Generaloberst*, I have not flown, Herr *Generaloberst* has seen the smoke trail on the ground. I took the liberty of a rolling check merely to ensure that all is in order for the display, Herr *Generaloberst*."

"And is it?"

"Everything is in excellent order!"

"Well in that case I saw nothing."

The Rechlin air display began. As part and parcel of the general demonstration, together with all new aircraft types and innovations including bomb containers, the rocket boosters were demonstrated. For the purposes of comparison, the Führer was shown a normal He 111H start alongside our He 111E with a 500 kg thrust Walter rocket under each wing. I had tested these machines along with the He 176 at Peenemünde since as a half-Heinkel half-RLM man I was not only there for the He 176, but for the 'special aircraft' too. In that respect I had the entire aviational paraphernalia of Peenemünde around my neck, since I was RLM's man at Peenemünde responsible for the aircraft.

A Peenemünde colleague flew the He 111 with the boosters, a Rechlin pilot handled the conventional He 111 in simultaneous take-offs. When the unassisted aircraft took off, the boostered He 111 was already close to 200 metres up. The roar of the rockets and the great trailing clouds of smoke gave the onlookers some impression of the power involved. The Führer was inspired and showed more interest in the rocket boosters than anything else.

Shortly before midday the Führer's car arrived at Roggentin bearing Hitler, Göring, Milch and Udet. I demonstrated to them first of all a standing test of the He 178 jet in which Dr von Ohain's turbine was installed. Although not yet ready for a flight but capable of a standing test we had decided to show off the machine. I sat in the

A team group photograph with Erich in the white flying suit.

Pre-demonstration flight preparations at Rechlin.

Hitler transfers from train to car for the final drive to the airfield.

cockpit while everybody else stood around. Dr von Ohain and Dr Heinkel delivered short addresses about the forthcoming maiden flight. This promised to be something and the Führer was undoubtedly interested. I will return to the He 178 later. Künzel, Bartelsen, Beilmann and I now proceeded to the He 176 parked on the airfield. We formed a line to one side of the machine, came to attention and saluted as the Führer came around the aircraft. Göring said something to him and Hitler looked at me directly. When Udet called my name I moved forward smartly to receive the Führer's handshake. It was a very firm grip, as was his custom, but he did not speak.

Hitler and Göring.

The German leaders meet von Ohain and Künzel.

The German Top Brass.

The Führer and his entourage then inspected the 176 closely. Hitler asked a few questions. He seemed extremely serious, in the past I had often had the opportunity to fly displays at which he was present, and on those occasions he had spoken to me, but I must say that I never saw him so grave as at the Roggentin show. It was only a few months before the outbreak of war: we had no suspicion of it then, but one assumed he already knew. Dr Heinkel and Udet gave explanations about the machine before everybody withdrew a few hundred metres. I climbed in and made the usual checks. At that moment *General-Ingenieur* Lucht turned up, looked into the cockpit, and shook my hand as I was buckling up. He wished me good luck, turned away and left. I had the feeling that all of them, Göring included, were being so nice to me because they thought this might be my death flight. On the other hand it might have been out of respect for my contribution to German aviation.

The demonstration flight begins.

Once the spectators were ready I received the signal to go. With full tanks and maximum all-up weight I needed 300 kms/hr to get the aircraft off the ground, for the tiny machine a remarkable speed! I banked, flew over the Führer at 200 metres, banked again for the touchdown, cut the fuel and swept in at 400 kms/hr. It was a very short flight. I had rather underestimated and shut off the fuel too soon, realizing at once that I would land short: I tried to restart the rocket but it refused! Meanwhile I had lost height very quickly but still had a lot of speed. Approaching the airfield boundary I saw a pile of bricks in my path. I pulled two levers and then the third in the desperate attempt to reignite the engine – with a loud report it restarted. At the perimeter, almost touching the ground the machine shot up fifty metres almost vertically and then dropped back. I shut off the fuel at once and at an airspeed of 250 kms/hr, tanks empty, made a fabulous landing.

Hitler and his entourage thought I had done it intentionally from bravado, of this there was no doubt in their minds. None of them suspected that I had been within a hair's breadth of disaster. My flight had been a successful one, however, and had made an impact. Therefore it was doubly successful! Only Heinkel and several others, Udet and Lucht, who understood the situation and were in the picture, had gasped with horror!

Meeting Hitler's party before the successful display of the He 176.

Once out of the aircraft a big Mercedes drove up and Hitler's adjutant Brückner told me that I should come to meet the Führer. We drove to the airfield boundary where he was looking at an exhibition

Hitler boards the train for his return journey.

of weapons. I stood with Brückner and watched Hitler board the big Mercedes with Göring for the drive to the Führer-train. When Göring returned we went to the officers' mess at Rechlin where lunch had been prepared. Udet and Milch were there. Immediately after dining the *Reichsmarschall* summoned me. He and Udet took me into an ante-room. Göring, leaning on a radiator, said: "Well, Herr Warsitz, I congratulate you. It went off extremely well! Tell me, what do you think of all the new contraptions?" That was the term he used, Kram, and I replied spontaneously, "Herr *Reichsmarschall*, it is no contraption. Guaranteed your personal and material support, I am convinced that in a few years there will be few propellered aircraft to be seen in the skies!"

He grinned, chewing on his Virginia cigar, slapped me on the shoulder, looked at Udet and said, "Here we have an optimist."

"Herr *Reichsmarschall,* not without justification," I replied.

Göring in a generous mood having awarded Erich 20,000 Reichsmarks for his flying display.

"To return to the subject of the rocket boosters, tell me how much time one would need to get a formation of, shall we say, around thirty aircraft equipped with boosters into the air?"

"From the word of command?"

"Yes, from the word of command."

"If the rocket booster ground crew is on the ball and there are no hang-ups, doing it as we are accustomed: half an hour."

At that he looked at Udet and said to me, "He has just told me forty-five minutes."

Udet made a gesture with his hand as if to say "I don't dispute what he says" and made no comment. In conclusion Göring said: "Herr Warsitz, since it went so successfully for you, I am awarding you 20,000 Reichsmarks for today's excellent display," and turning to Udet added, "Ernst, you know what I mean, out of the special fund." I thanked him and was dismissed. Nobody learned about this conversation except Dr Heinkel, but even he was not aware of what I am about to recount next, and with regard to which Udet swore me to silence...

Erich in the centre wearing the white suite after returning to Peenemünde from Rechlin.

CHAPTER ELEVEN

The Reich Chancellery

Three days after the Rechlin display I received from Udet the command to present myself at 0900 next morning at RLM. I was to wear a dark suit. At the appointed hour I reported. Udet asked, "Do you know what it is about? You are to see the Führer." He supplied a few rules on protocol and asked me to return to RLM to see him as soon as I left the Reich Chancellery. Next I went before a gold-braided administration official at RLM who looked me up and down and gave me a few more rules on protocol. Then he asked, "Are you a Party member?"

"Of course," I lied. Actually I had no political affiliation, politics never interested me.

"So where is your party badge?"

"I left it at home, I never wear it." He rummaged through a drawer and pinned one on my lapel. A little later I drove to the Reich Chancellery and went through a succession of three ante-rooms before I was received finally by Hitler's adjutant Brückner. He had a few words with me and then said, "OK, let's go in." I had been advised beforehand that I would be searched for a weapon, but I have to say they must have forgotten. I was never asked to submit to a search. At the door Brückner said, "Just one moment!" He went into the Führer's study and reappeared immediately to escort me inside. Announcing "*Flugkapitän* Warsitz!" he left at once. I was alone with the Führer. Hitler, who was sitting behind his enormous desk, arose and, after my bow came around the desk to approach me. I bowed again and received his handshake. I was directed to a corner furnished with a sofa, two armchairs and a small table. There were no ashtrays anywhere in the room, apparently nobody ever smoked here, and he certainly did not offer me a cigarette.

I had been advised, 'When you meet the Führer, do not avoid his gaze!' That was not difficult, I had spoken to him often and was not accustomed to looking away no matter who looked at me. At first he was awfully serious looking but when I said the name of my home town, Hattingen in the Ruhr, he brightened and said with a smile, "From my Hochburg!" Hattingen, since 1926 a Nazi stronghold, he knew well from the era of the street struggles. He had stayed there very often, in his windcheater in our one tavern, now called the 'Hitler Cellar'. This broke the spell. In the course of our conversation he asked many advanced technical questions. This surprised me and I did not answer them as if he were a layman. He showed great interest in both the rocket and jet engines, and especially the He 178, since jet turbines promised greater speeds and endurance, and were suitable for bombers. The 18-month wait which I forecast for the aircraft to be ready to enter series production seemed to him to be excessive. He appeared convinced that the imminent war would end for us victoriously within a year. From this observation, his later decision to stop the development is understandable.

After 20 minutes – it was a long talk – Brückner came to announce the arrival of the *Reichsmarschall* and Udet. I was surprised what an upright figure Göring cut with his marshall's baton. After the usual greetings Udet suggested I should drive to the RLM and await him there. The Führer accompanied me to the door, told me to take care and wished me the traditional 'safe landing' – *Hals und Beinbruch*. Very impressed, of course, I drove to RLM. When Udet returned I made a full report of what Hitler had told me. This conference had to remain secret. Udet ordered me never to mention it, not even to Heinkel – he only learned of it from me much later – so that nothing would be made public and the attention of our enemies would not be called to Peenemünde and prejudice our project. That was one reason. The other, as Udet pointed out, was that many other Rechlin pilots who had likewise achieved something special at the air display would feel snubbed. At that he said, "I congratulate you for your rise in salary. The Führer has ordered your income and insurances doubled. My heartiest best wishes!"

What! I was insured for over a million! "It is not possible, Herr *Generaloberst!*" I protested. How had this come about? After I had flown the He 176 for Hitler, he went with Udet and Heinkel to see a display at the bomb arsenal. On the way he asked what I earned. Neither knew and when he pressed Udet for an answer he came up with a figure out of thin air. Hitler gave the impression he thought it too little. I have no idea if Dr Heinkel was aware of the respectable sums I had received from him: when the 176 project was set up I had been placed at his disposal by the RLM and Udet as a test pilot for the machine. Udet said: "Heinkel must make you a contract for the 176, but before you sign it, I want to see it first!"

When the 176 was still being built, Heinkel's technical director Professor Hertel had given me the proposal for a contract. I showed this to Udet. He read it and hit the roof. "What a piece of shit. And you want to sign this? You're crazy. Everything you've done for a few miserable marks! You have no idea of the danger you have been courting, and will do so in the future. Those there in Rostock want to shit all over you!" I was astounded. "There is no question of this," he went on "go into the other room and draw up your own contract, then show it to me."

"Herr *Generaloberst*, I cannot do this," I replied, "I am a novice at that sort of thing, and would not know where to begin."

"See Oberst Pendele, he will sort you one out."

"But Herr Generaloberst, what does Oberst Pendele know about it? Obviously, he is a good lawyer, but he would not have a clue what figures to put down. If you give me some idea, then I will happily convey them to Pendele."

With his violet pencil he struck out 5,000 Reichsmarks for the first flight and substituted 50,000. He raised the reward for every 100 kms/hr airspeed, and for every flight by 500 Reichmarks and so on. Then he slid the contract back across the table. I could hardly believe my eyes. "Now take it to Pendele!" I went to the adjutant. "Herr *Oberst*, the chief has sent me, you should set this in the correct form." He did it and when I showed Udet he said, "Now go to negotiate this with Heinkel!"

A few days later I informed Heinkel that Udet wanted to see the contract before I signed it and Heinkel said, "Yes, show me, is it in order?"

Erich seen in the middle facing Göring in the Reich headquarters.

"Herr Doktor, Udet was not absolutely in agreement with your terms and he made me prepare another one with a few minor changes. Here it is."

As Heinkel read it he almost fell off his stool. Reviewing the figures he turned pale, looked up at the ceiling and said, "Who in the world has got money like this?"

"I had nothing to do with it," I assured him. He took his fountain pen, signed the document and said laconically, "It's all the same, Fatty will pay it." Fatty – der Dicke – was Göring. Heinkel never had to pay a pfennig and invoiced it all to RLM. The contract was agreed in the following format:

First Flight: 50,000 Reichsmarks
Speed of 400 kms/hr: 20,000 RM:
For each additional 100 kms/hr an additional 20,000 RM
    up to and including 900 kms/hr:
Speed of 1000 kms/hr: 50,000 RM.

Furthermore I received 500 RM per flight from the beginning irrespective of whether the flight was a flight or short leap, or whatever. Additionally I received remuneration corresponding to the highest grade of RLM test pilot retrospective to my first day at Kummersdorf, as an employee of Heinkel, and from when Peenemünde was built, as chief pilot, highest grade at Peenemünde. In all in 1939 alone I earned 600,000 Reichsmarks, and the year before not much less. (At the time a top engineer in German industry could expect to earn 10,000 Reichsmarks annually). I believe I am the biggest money-earner, as a pilot, in the history of aviation who neither wanted it nor had to bargain for it.

CHAPTER TWELVE

Heinkel 178 – The Most Secret Development

After what we had learnt from the He 176, an aircraft which had been developed in close cooperation with RLM, Heinkel was now a little bitter at not receiving the support he expected and needed, for after the first flights it seemed interest in it had died away. Not all people in the decisive area at RLM had lost interest, but war was looming and there were other things to think about. From the aviation point of view the He 176 was undoubtedly the forerunner of the entire turbine and rocket engine development, for everything rose from the foundations we laid with that project.

At that time I was often at RLM. I remember returning from there very depressed one day and saying to Heinkel that RLM considered all our work just 'an impressive plaything'. A lot had been going wrong and it prompted me to suggest to Heinkel that we should close the books on it all. He raged at me: "We shall close the books on nothing! Is everything we have achieved to go to the dogs?" He added angrily, "Warsitz, the day will soon come when we shall put the first jet aircraft on the doorstep of those gentlemen! Everything will look different, and we shall also win the absolute world speed record for Germany!"

Long previously I had become accustomed to the strange whining howl of an engine at Heinkel's, the test runs of his first jet turbine. In order to relate this story from the beginning I have to go back a few years to when von Braun asked Heinkel if he would place an aircraft at his disposal. In 1936 Professor Pohl of Göttingen University wrote to Heinkel, whom he knew: "I have here a very capable and innovative man who is working on a jet turbine. We cannot help him any more here because our means are limited. Would you be interested?"

Heinkel, fired with enthusiasm as usual, replied at once, "Send him over!" And so it came about that he installed Hans Joachim Pabst von Ohain, the developer, the inventor one might almost say, of the turbine, and made available to him a laboratory at the Rostock works.

Pabst von Ohain:

My interest in jet engines began in about 1933. I found that the elegance of flying was spoiled by the enormous vibrations and noise from the piston engine/propeller combination. I came to the conclusion that a constant work process, i.e. constant compression, combustion, expansion, would have great advantages. I set myself three criteria for my research: the greatest simplicity, least risk during development and much lighter weight than an equivalent piston engine. Thus I chose a quite simple engine, a radial compressor with a radial turbine. I made a few broad calculations and established that the probable weight reduction could be as much as two-thirds of the piston engine. My biggest problem was to sell this idea and I thought it would be best to build a model first of all. A very good automobile mechanic – the type you do not find today – whom I had known for ages, Max Hahn, taught me very much about automobile engines. He had at his disposal all the tooling machinery of a fair-sized repair shop. I showed him my sketches and he suggested some simplifications and changes so that he could build the model with the tools at hand. Hahn reduced the costs to within my financial means.

Afterwards I explained my theory to Professor Pohl and showed him some photos of the model. Pohl was a physicist and engines were not his area of expertise, but very generously he allowed me to set up the model engine in the courtyard of the Institute, putting an electric motor and other instruments at my disposal to enable me to make the first cold runs. At ignition garish long flames came from the turbine. My engine looked like a new kind of flame-thrower.

I was very disappointed for I knew immediately what this meant: the combustion chamber arrangement did not work, as the soot traces showed: the flame was burning inside the turbine and had somehow stabilized there and not in the combustion chamber. I knew that this was the end for my project because I could not engineer the chamber development.

Professor Pohl was absolutely fantastic. He said: "One thing you should never forget, I have examined your theory closely, it is sound and your calculations are correct, but you cannot develop the combustion unit without industrial help. Give me the name of somebody in industry to whom you would like to go and I will write him a letter." I said, "Heinkel has the reputation of being keen on speed, fast cars and fast aircraft, and he doesn't back away from new ideas. Heinkel is where I want to go." Heinkel invited me to come at once and gave me a very generous licensing contract.

As already mentioned, at the end of 1936, almost overnight Heinkel built a special hall near the Wasserhalle, alongside the giant factory halls, for the development of the He 176. It was there too that von Ohain worked on his turbine. Few ever entered, and the tightest guard was kept over it by factory security. Only a small circle knew what was afoot, and not even they were allowed to enter unless wearing the special badge!

Pabst von Ohain:

The whole project was named Special Development, and Engineer Gundermann came as design leader with two or three engineers. He brought honest-to-goodness know-how and very ingenious light-construction techniques, and worked out all the stress factors. Gundermann, Hahn and I made a very small but extremely good and competent team.

Under the pressure of aiming to bring a combustion chamber of unknown endurance to flight readiness, I came upon the idea of separating the turbine problem from the combustion chamber problem by using a hydrogen fuel. As a physicist, I knew of course that the diffusion and combustion speed of gaseous hydrogen was substantially greater than that of petrol.

Gundermann, Hahn and I did the sketches post-haste and without any pre-trials the combustion installation worked wonderfully. Because of the small torque inertia the apparatus worked almost like a motor.

In February 1937 the first turbine ran on the test stand in the 'special development' hall at Rostock with the typical howl known to everybody today. Initially these test runs were never made during working hours but in the evening or at night when only half the labour force would be present, because the engine noise was clearly audible outside the hall. Such was the secrecy.

It was some considerable time before von Ohain had advanced the He-S3 turbine sufficiently for it to be flight-tested. From a scientific point of view it should not be forgotten that it was something absolutely novel and could be expected to have the usual run of setbacks and breakdowns.

Pabst von Ohain:

Now we could work systematically on the construction of the combustion chamber. We had a programme, Max Hahn did phenomenal work and not only carried out the scheduled combustion programme but developed many ideas of which some led to important patents. We were now working on a machine capable of powering an aircraft, the forerunner of the He-S3B. I had intended to put the combustion chamber between the compressor and the turbine, as we had done with the hydrogen unit, but Hahn suggested putting it ahead of them, which was an excellent idea. The machine could be built more compact and had the aerodynamic advantage that the 'residual swirl' mixed in with the hot flame gases.

The turbines would explode on the test stand initially after about 10,000 revolutions and fly through the air in a thousand shreds, this was perfectly normal! When the engine was ready we planned a basic trial flight. Naturally as the appointed specialist for all rocket projects at Heinkel I wanted to fly it. As with the von Braun or Walter rocket motors, I would fly using the turbine as a supplementary engine. We used an He 118, a heavy dual-seater reconnaissance aircraft, as the carrier. The aircraft had high clearance, the large undercarriage giving

An He 118.

us the space clear of the ground which we needed to instal the turbine below the fuselage. I made a few flights with this machine, but not alone: Künzel flew with me. Once in the air by the conventional engine Künzel started the turbine. We measured and observed the additional thrust it provided. It could be throttled from the beginning. On the third flight it caught fire. I was able to land safely but the engine and aircraft burnt out, and that was an end to the flight trials for the time being.

Meanwhile Heinkel had summoned his whole team of designers, technical directors, stress analysts and such people to announce: "We want to build a special aircraft with jet drive! The RLM is not to know anything about the 178. I take full responsibility!" The He 176 had been developed almost from the outset at the instigation and with the approval of RLM, the He 178 was not! The development was pursued by Heinkel without the knowledge of RLM and a short while later the small machine would open the Jet Age.

Once the second turbine, the He-S3A, was ready at the beginning of 1939 it was installed into the body of the He 178 airframe designed meanwhile by Heinkel. I had played a decisive and also technical role in the work. The machine was a shoulder-wing airplane of light metal construction, the fuselage of Dural. It was built with safety in mind, had a wide wheelbase, large brakes and bore no similarities to the He 176. I specified the instrumentation, because in the air all devolved on to me, and the good von Ohain made the changes just as von Braun or Walter would have done. The engine had two fuel pumps, but the supply system was a sickly child. The worst difficulties were caused by uncertainty as to the best materials for the endurance of the turbine blades, and the insufficient thrust. These were the reasons why it was not risked in flight early on.

Until then Heinkel had succeeded in keeping the entire project secret from RLM. In accordance with his wish I had said nothing. Nevertheless something filtered through to them, and the RLM took a dim view of my not having said something to them: since visitors from RLM were not allowed into the 'special aircraft' hall there was understandable friction between the RLM technical experts and Heinkel. It was an awkward situation for me because I was an RLM-man but represented at the same time the interests of Heinkel. I can still hear Heinkel's words today: "What we are doing here is the business of nobody else: it must remain between us until we can provide the RLM with a demonstration flight!" The cat was now out of the bag, however, and so we decided to show the He 178 to the Führer at Roggentin on 3 July 1939 alongside the He 176. As already mentioned it was only a standing display because the thrust of the He-S3A turbine was not powerful enough for flight.

Pabst von Ohain:

> Now what was the reason why the turbine was still not as good as we had hoped? We experimented with various combinations to modify the compressor diffuser and turbine nozzle vanes to increase thrust sufficiently to qualify the aircraft for the first flight demonstration. This gave us 450kg thrust, in my opinion 500 kg. We found that a small diffuser behind the engine with a collar and splitter to divert flows functioned better than a high speed flow through the entire tube. The final result of the changes was the He-S3B. Engineer Gundermann worked hard to use the static pressure, limited in the He 178 by the engine

He-S3B Turbine. (Deutsches Museum – München)

frontal area. He hated the adversely long air inlet and jet pipe and argued for a twin-jet version, but nobody wanted to hear this at the time. It would have been too expensive and Heinkel preferred less power and a simple aircraft.

After years of work, hundreds of test runs, eternal modifications and setbacks, the standing tests slowly began to pall and we were all keen to see the result in flight. Heinkel asked me to make the maiden flight at Rostock-Marienehe (Peenemünde is often wrongly stated in modern accounts). At first I declined: "Dear Doktor, it is too dangerous to make the first flight from your relatively short strip. Better at Peenemünde, we have an extra 300 metres there for the take-off!"

"Warsitz, how can you say such a thing," he retorted. "First Peenmünde will know everything, and then everybody will know everything! No, it must be made here!"

Not long afterwards von Ohain was ready enough for us to dare flying the 178 with his He-S3B at the beginning of August 1939. One day Heinkel rang me and asked: "Warsitz, how much longer?"

"As far as I am concerned we have been ready for ages, but Ohain is still tinkering with it."

Heinkel thought so too. "But is it ready?"

"I would say so."

"When would you like to fly?"

"Why not tomorrow?"

"No," he replied, "'the day after'."

At the Heinkel works far less attention could now be paid to secrecy. It had become less important, for whereas something could be kept secret in a cellar or some other hideaway, one could hardly do so once the thing was flying. When we flew the He 176 at Peenemünde, the people sunning themselves on the beach at Zinnowitz, 15 kilometres away suddenly heard a tremendous thunder in the sky, and everybody looked. That put an end to the secrecy!

Therefore the maiden flight was set intentionally for 0400 because nobody would be at work then and the people of Rostock still safely abed. We knew that they would scramble up – later confirmed – once they heard this aircraft scream past with its unique engine sound, but by then it would be long gone, and they would have seen nothing.

CHAPTER THIRTEEN

The World's First
Jet Flight

The He 178 was a completely new type of aircraft from airframe to engine, and for the pilot it was not simply a matter of getting in and flying off. Being a heavy smoker I would light up a few extra cigarettes before such flights, and it was wearing especially when, settled in the cockpit after the ready signal, the engine was checked over one last time and somebody would call out: "Stop, call it off, there's a loose valve here!" Then I would have to disembark again. This made one edgy!

Of course there were many question marks, for although the turbine had run standing tests day and night, one never knew how safe it would be after the latest modifications. I could do nothing about that. I had followed the progress of the machine from the drawing board and been involved in it. I knew what had to be done now and was quite philosophical in that respect. It was not the first prototype I had ever flown. I knew the dangers, but was inwardly strong, and my motto was: 'If something happens in the air and I have enough altitude, come what may I have my parachute.' I had had to bale out nine times in my career, why should the tenth be unsuccessful? Admittedly one imagines things, but that is not fear – when one is fearful one cannot be calm, and with new machinery like this things can go wrong with a second's inattention, or switching on a fraction of a second too late! But I wobbled, that I have to admit!

The war with Poland was only days away, and flak batteries at readiness surrounded the Heinkel works at Rostock–Marienehe. Flak guns were set up everywhere inside the works premises, and also at the neighbouring Arado aircraft factory. They had orders to 'report every aircraft to flak central control' and some were even expected to 'shoot them all down!' If they did, I would be amongst the victims! The orders were actually to shoot at any aircraft not clearly identified, which included my own, since it bore no registration markings for reasons of secrecy and made a strange engine noise. The day previous to the flight I obtained from the flak commander a plan of their battery layout to know the gun positions and firing angles: right along the flight path – there was only a concrete airstrip at Marienehe on the W-E axis and the flak was stationed either side of it. I would have to fly over them. I noted down: 'After lifting off, must fly very low over the flak positions and keep low until safe to ascend.' I did not know how the flak organization worked, and so I was hoping that they would still be asleep at four in the morning and stood down from their batteries.

An extremely rare photo of the Heinkel He 178 part seen to the right of the car.

On Sunday 27 August 1939 we were ready. It was a glorious morning, calm and still. The machine was towed to the apron for take-off. I could see no activity amongst the flak people. Because of the great secrecy we had to keep the machine away from the works field, which meant I could not carry out the usual rolling tests. Like the Me 176, the 178 had major differences from a conventional aircraft: the rudder was only effective at higher speeds shortly before take-off so that I would have to use the brakes to keep her straight on the runway. Immediately before the flight I roll-tested the aircraft over a short stretch and noted that the brakes were not only adequate for correcting the heading but superb! The 178 was much larger than the 176, heavier and had at least a 1.3 wheelbase. In the 178 I could sit up correctly: the pilot seat was so located that the intake shaft for the turbine did not obstruct it. Narrow, obviously, but no comparison to the 176 which needed a shoe-horn to fit the pilot in!

Showing the cockpit area of the 178.

Heinkel himself and his colleagues looked with some apprehension at the circuit, for meanwhile it had been recognized that the aircraft of the future was not the rocket aircraft but the jet with its longer flight time and greater margin of safety. I checked the rudder movements, tested the turbine at various revolutions, the pump pressures, temperatures and much besides before giving the ground crew the signal to close the canopy. Dr Heinkel came to the machine, shook my hand and, obviously edgy and excited, wished me *Hals und Beinbruch* – safe landing! He looked very serious.

This photo shows the substantial undercarriage.

Side view of the 178.

I moved the throttle levers gently forward. As the aircraft began to roll I was initially rather disappointed at the thrust, for she did not shoot forward as the 176 had done, but moved off slowly. By the 300-metre mark she was moving very fast. The 176 was much more spectacular, more agile, faster and more dangerous. The 178 on the other hand was more like a utility aircraft and resembled a conventional aircraft except for the chicanery – the 'Christmas tree decorations' as we called them.

In this machine I felt completely safe and had no worries that my fuel tanks would be dry within a minute. She was wonderfully easy to hold straight, and then she lifted off. Despite several attempts I could not retract the undercarriage. It was not important, all that mattered was that she flew. The rudder and all flaps worked almost normally, the turbine howled. It was glorious to fly, the morning was windless,

This photo shows the substantial undercarriage.

the sun low on the horizon. My air speed indicator registered 600 kms/hr, and that was the maximum Schwärzler had warned me. Therefore I throttled back since I habitually accepted the advice of experienced aeronautical engineers. The tanks were not full and, contrary to custom, I did not want to gain altitude for a parachute jump should things go awry. It was supposed to be a short flight. At 300 to 400 metres altitude I banked cautiously left – rudder effect not quite normal, the machine hung to the left a little, but I held her easily with the control stick, she turned a little more and everything looked good.

After flying a wide circuit my orders were to land at once, this had been hammered into me, but now I felt the urge to go round again. I increased speed and thought, 'Ach! I will!' Below I could see the team waving at me. On the second circuit – I had been in the air six minutes – I told myself 'Finish off!' and began the landing. The turbine obeyed my movement of the throttle even though a fuel pump had failed, as I knew from my instruments and later during the visual checks. Because the airfield was so small for such flights I was a little worried about the landing because we did not know for certain the safe landing speed: we knew the right approach, gliding and landing speeds in theory, but not in practice, and they did not always coincide.

I swept down on the heading for the runway. I was too far forward and did not have the fuel for another circuit. Now I would have to take my chances with the landing, losing altitude by side-slipping. I was flying an unfamiliar, new type of aircraft at high speed near the ground and I was not keen on side-slipping. It was certainly a little risky, but the alternative was overshooting into the River Warnow. Such an ending, soaking wet at four on a Sunday morning, appealed less. The onlookers were horror-struck at the manoeuvre. They were sure I was going to spread the aircraft over the airfield. But the well-built kite was very forgiving. I restored her to the correct attitude just before touching down, made a wonderful landing and pulled up just short of the Warnow.

Landing safely after the first jet flight.

The first jet flight in history had succeeded! The tension broke, everybody was jubilant. I got out of the cockpit, the ground crew bore the overjoyed Dr Heinkel and myself on their shoulders, and after a short debriefing in the officers' mess we drank a toast to the first flight pointing the way to the future direction of aviation. Heinkel rang Udet. At this early hour it took some time to get him to the receiver. Heinkel announced: *"Flugkapitän* Warsitz had just landed successfully after making the world's first jet flight!" Udet congratulated him, asked to speak to me, offered his congratulations and then said, "And now back to bed".

His reaction disappointed us a little for we thought rightly that by our success we had conquered a world and heralded in a new epoch. The results I reported from the first flight of the 178 were evaluated and further modifications made to the aircraft. These were mainly to the rudder in connection with the steering forces and so on, like the 176 they were too strong. The 178 also did not seem too stable in the longitudinal axis. When Dr Heinkel revealed his secret achievement to the RLM, he naturally expected an invitation to display his success in decisive quarters. He was soon sobered in his hopes, for with the outbreak of war the following Friday, Berlin had other things on its plate. At the end of September, however, he was given a promise that Göring, Milch, Udet and Lucht would be pleased to watch an exhibition flight at Marienehe on 1 November 1939.

Celebration after the epic flight.

CHAPTER FOURTEEN

The Exhibition Flight

On 1 November 1939 Milch, Udet, Lucht and entourage arrived by Ju 52 at Rostock-Marienehe. Göring was not with them. We had readied the 178 and after greeting our visitors proceeded to the machine. Dr Heinkel and his team delivered a few technical reports then retreated. I got into the machine. After starting but before taking off – as mentioned the airstrip was too short and the dyke embankment of the River Warnow was incorporated as its far end – a fuel pump failed. I noticed this at once from the noise and loss of power. In an emergency I could have done a circuit with one pump but there was a danger of being underpowered which could have led to a crash. I decided at once to abort take-off, I shut down the engine, stepped hard on the brakes and intentionally made a ground spin to prevent the aircraft toppling over the embankment. During this manoeuvre a tyre burst which made the ground spin look more dangerous to the spectators than it was.

Dr Heinkel drove up in his car to enquire into the problem.

"Shit, the fuel pump failed again."

"Oh God oh God," he cried, "what are we going to tell them?"

"Leave that to me!" I returned with him in the car to face the generals. "Well, Warsitz, what went wrong?" Milch asked.

"A tyre burst."

"Yes, but you had already lifted off, hadn't you?"

"Just as I was taking off the tyre burst, and you know, Herr *Generalfeldmarschall*, if one knows a tyre has gone – it has happened to me before – one does not risk a landing at speed! Since it was still possible I chose to brake and do a spin, but at least the machine is still in one piece!"

Lucht, who was standing behind Milch, grinned and narrowed an eye. He had seen through it. Milch made no response. Perhaps he was being decent enough not to show that he knew I had lied. (The purpose of this lie about the fuel pump was to prevent the generals, who were looking for a problem from the outset, from seizing upon the breakdown to argue that the development was insufficiently mature to recommend series production. Author's note.) In any case there was a bad atmosphere amongst them now, and the exhibition flight, by which Heinkel had set so much store, seemed to have been lost, but he managed to interest them in some new things he had in the Wasserhalle, including an He 177, and then invited them to breakfast in the mess. Meanwhile, up to our elbows in oil, we set about installing a new feed pump and told Heinkel on the quiet: "We'll see to it that it's repaired, keep them here."

"How long will you need?"

"At the most two hours. We hope to have it done by then, but we're not certain." Heinkel was naturally encouraged by this and he kept them talking. Finally they emerged for their flight to Berlin.

"Just a moment, *meine Herren*, you wanted to see the 178 fly?"

"Yes, but surely it will not be flying again today?"

"Well of course. It was only a burst tyre. In fact it is ready!" He spoke with a certainty that took my breath away.

I climbed back into the machine and took off, flew several circuits, one over their heads, passing them to one side, fairly low down, probably at 700 kms/hr to judge by the engine noise. At that moment Udet and Lucht both complained: "That crazy Warsitz should land, what does he want to stay up there so long for?" I made a fantastic landing and pulled up a few metres from where they stood: they had to spring apart a bit, and then I stopped before them. Not much brake, no ground spin, nothing. A complete success!

Dr Heinkel beamed, having now achieved what he wanted, for everything depended on this demonstration. He was certainly counting on the RLM financing him, for the development to date had cost him a pretty pfennig, and

The 178 after the successful demonstration flight.

we were all looking into future skies and could see only jet aircraft there. There remained, however, no time for discussion or recognition, and our visitors boarded their Ju 52 and flew off. They were in a hurry and had not even arrived in good humour. One felt the tension between Milch and Heinkel. This was mainly for the clandestine manner of the development. Milch warned me that I was an RLM-man and did not belong to Heinkel, which I should bear in mind. I justified my silence on our having to take into account the great difficulties and delays over the He 176 because RLM had made completely senseless technical demands.

"That is Udet's business," Milch replied. After their departure we were all bitterly disappointed. Was that it? A heap of congratulations and nothing else? Did nobody realize what we had achieved here?

CHAPTER FIFTEEN

Further Development Stopped

I shall never forget the Führer-Directive ordering all developments not ready for mass-production within a year to be suspended with immediate effect. All of us, but especially me fought alongside Udet for permission to continue, but somewhere along the way Udet gave up and the whole thing ground to a halt. I had been hoping to set an absolute world speed record of over 1000 kms/hr, not with the He 176-V1 of course, because it was a DIY job not suitable for it. The Heinkel stress analysts and Schwärzler, chief designer, all warned, 'Not above 600, that is her limit.'

All the modifications to the V1 were applied to the V2 so that we could really have pulled out all the stops with her and exceeded 1000 kms/hr. The V2 had a strengthened von Braun rocket engine and was capable of vertical ascent because the thrust was greater than the total weight. We even discussed a record flight as the possibility was within reach.

Because of the need to tank up with rocket fuel the flight would have been measured by the Stettin flak rangefinder crew on the banks of the Peene near Peenemünde. Registering the claim would have been very difficult but Heinkel was keen to go ahead with it*. He had accordingly initiated the procedure for an international record flight attempt, which had to be reported beforehand to the Swiss authorities and two sworn witnesses nominated. This would have been a major obstacle, because the application required the aircraft type, hp, kind

---

*At that time Germany had four living world record holders in aviation, in itself a world record. They were: 11.11.1937 Dr Hermann Wurster (Bf 109E) 611.004 km/hr (world record for land aircraft): 5.6.1938 Ernst Udet (He 100) 634.73 km/hr (world record for land aircraft): 30.3.1939 Hans Dieterle (He 100 V8) 746.606 km/hr (absolute world air speed record) and 26.4.1939 Fritz Wendel (Me 209 V1) 755.138 km/hr (absolute world air speed record). Heinkel's ambition to take the absolute air speed record would undoubtedly have been doubly sweet if he could have robbed Messerschmitt of the title.

of engine to be declared, and this would not be possible with the 176 for reasons of secrecy. Heinkel thought that Udet and Göring might let it go through with certain restrictions. Theoretically the whole procedure for the record flight was in place, so far had our intentions advanced, but the war came a few months, half a year, too soon!

In consequence the He 176 did not end its career as we all expected when we said: "One day this bird will break its own neck." Instead, in 1940, it was packed into a special steel crate, sealed and welded, and taken to the Aviation Museum in Berlin for eventual display as the first manned rocket aircraft in the world to fly. It was the end of the 176, for the crate was destroyed together with the museum during the great air raid on Berlin and the 176 disappeared for ever into the world beyond.

After its display before Milch, Udet and Lucht, the He 178 made several more flights, but not very many, and shortly afterwards I dedicated myself fully to my work as chief pilot at Peenemünde-West and as an instructor in France.

CHAPTER SIXTEEN

France 1941 – Instructing the Front Squadrons

At the end of the French campaign the bomber squadrons received the rocket boosters but had no sufficient training in their use. A terrible accident occurred in which a pilot, a young *Leutnant* and former Peenemünde test pilot, lost his life. The tragedy happened at Eindhoven, Holland, and involved a Ju 88 armed with two bombs for a raid on England. Shortly after the pilot began his take-off run, one of the two boosters failed, but he let the other burn instead of shutting it down, probably because he thought he could still get up on the survivor. The machine spun on the ground and roared into a clearing of a pine forest near the airfield where it came to a stop. For an unknown reason one of the two bombs then exploded destroying everything forward except the pilot seat, after which the whole machine caught fire. The pilot was found roasted, body inside but head outside the aircraft, as if he had been in the act of getting out. The burnt wreck was left where it stood, and on Christmas Eve 1940 RLM sent me to Eindhoven to investigate and report back. I concluded that the cause was pilot error. If the pilot had shut down his engines and cut out the working booster, allowing the aircraft to roll to a stop, he would have had plenty of room and nothing would have happened.

Shortly afterwards a similar case occurred which had worse consequences. At Nantes, France, a Ju 88 was taking off for a raid on England. One of the two rocket boosters failed when he had three metres altitude. He allowed the surviving booster to continue its burn. This caused the aircraft to turn in the air and crash into the control tower. All eight 250-kg bombs aboard then exploded. The crew of the Ju 88 and the 15 occupants of the tower lost their lives.

An He 111 in the background as discussions concerning the accidents take place.

These accidents were the prelude to the decision of the *Luftwaffe* General Staff to ban operations using the rockets. The squadrons also refused to fly with them, considering them unreliable. By then I had flown between 400 and 500 test flights, some under the most difficult conditions. Incidents occurring in the early flights were not due to boosters exploding or other such defects since they remained intact. The units were in every respect operational and defect-free except for rare shut-downs, and so Udet ordered me to fly with a Peenemünde engineer to France to train and calm the crews. Another nice little job!

Our first port of call was Nantes, where all the Generals of the Air Fleet had assembled to hear my verdict on the awful collision of the Ju 88 into the control tower. I explained that all the incidents were the result of pilot error. I had made about 500 flights under much more difficult circumstances and without a single disaster. I asked for a Ju 88 to be made ready to fly. I made a 'Stuka' nose dive which was not supposed to be demonstrated to front fliers. Then I made a second flight in which I switched on the rocket boosters at 20 metres altitude. Then I told them: "As most of your flights are over England at night, you will certainly be interested in the possibility of finding out what one can do at night in a Ju 88 with take-off aids!"

Next I made a night flight and took off conventionally. At 200 metres altitude I flew over the airfield at a decent speed, not bombed-up of course, opened the throttles, started the rockets and looped the loop. I had tried this previously on tests, but not at night! That naturally took the ground from under the feet of the Air Fleet and its Generals! I showed them that all occurrences were attributable to pilot error. All doubt now began to dispel.

The following day there occurred another interesting event which afforded me an insight into the problems at Nantes. The squadron commander was a Major Emig who had earlier been employed at RLM. The Ministry had got him his pilot's licence at Staaken or Rangsdorf – as was usual then – and given him command of a bomber squadron. I was acquainted with him. He had made a few training flights with me and he was pleased I had come. He poured out his heart and confided that he shit himself every time he led his squadron on a raid over England. "I can speak to you frankly. You know that I have no flight experience but have to lead my squadron over England. Some of my wingmen are experienced pilots who cover me in all situations. But I have to fly!" Emig was right. I knew several of his pilots who had come from DVS, already highly decorated and who also confided to me: "Emig is a fantastic guy, the best type of comrade, but he should really stay at home and let us go alone. That would be far better!" This was not allowed then, the squadron commanders had to fly. Emig was later transferred out and went to the Eastern Front. While mining a port he came in too low, his mine hit a quay, exploded and knocked him down. He received a posthumous Knight's Cross.

But now to the interesting insight I gained. After I had demonstrated the night flight, Major Emig scheduled some conventional night flights for his Ju 88 pilots. The *Luftwaffe* Generals were all away. Emig and I stood in idle conversation with a number of senior officers watching the take-offs. A number of pilots took off, did a circuit and then waited to land. While chatting I noticed suddenly the navigation lights of a Ju 88 coming in between two hangars at an altitude lower than their roof. I said to Emig: "What's this then?" The aircraft touched down, bounced up 10 metres, touched down again, bounced up again and so on. The Ju 88, known to have a very strong undercarriage, held out.

"Herr Emig, I should like to speak to that pilot," I requested. When he arrived I asked him, "Tell me, did you just make that landing?"

"Jawohl!"

"And where did you come in from?"

"Well, over there."

"Do you know what height you were at?"

"No, I cannot say exactly."

"Apart from your pig's breakfast of a landing, you came in between those two hangars. If I had wanted to do that I might not have made it, but you were lucky. What type of licence do you have?"

"A C-licence!"

"And what night-flying training?"

"None yet."

"None at all?"

"No," he said, "that was my first night flight, apart from a couple of landings in the dark which I had to do for my C-licence!"

I thanked him, and Emig explained that all the people he was getting were just like this pilot, no night-flying experience, and that he could not train them here – i.e. make a few night flights – by order of the *Luftwaffe* General Staff to save fuel! These young men were then sent to bomb England at night. All the new men received by Emig's squadron fitted in this category. And that was in 1941!

To return to squadron training. At various airfields I repeated what I had demonstrated at Nantes and Eindhoven: after a few exhibition flights I took along a competent pilot whom I knew, showed off in the aircraft and then let him handle the training. He instructed everybody in the boosters with the result that the objections to their use were quickly forgotten. In subsequent months I repeated these visits to France frequently and soon I found that the squadrons I visited would not fly *without* the rocket boosters.

He 111s with rocket-assisted take-off, depart for a raid over England.

CHAPTER SEVENTEEN

Heinkel He 280 or Messerschmitt Me 262

I t is always forgotten, or not correctly reported, that the He 178 was a purely experimental aircraft with the first jet engine. After the successful flights and experience gained there was nothing left to do but begin planning for a new kind of operational warplane. Heinkel slipped into gear automatically, from the designers and stress analysts to the constructors, and so the He 280 was conceived. The nose wheel was indispensable, for at take-off the machine was then easy to keep on its heading without danger of it straying laterally. I mentioned previously that this could only be cured with the He 176 and 178 by braking on the opposite side to the veer and that despite the necessary fine touch, especially with the He 176, it led to countless dangerous ground spins and also to wingtip contact with the ground and resultant wing or tailplane damage.

At the time of the first He 178 flights there was no compelling reason to consider twin-engine designs since we were focused on experimental flight with one turbine. Apart from the turbine breakdowns and problems with the supply pumps everything proceeded unusually smoothly for a new engine development of that kind. Testing was still in its early stages and everybody knew that the road would be a long one until the engine would be reliable enough for series production. From the summer of 1939 the He-S6 turbine was being built and at the beginning of 1940 Heinkel was asked by RLM to develop the He 280. The aircraft had to be fitted with two He-S8 turbines slung below the wings in order to avoid the intake and exhaust shafts we had in the He 178 airframe. Since the engines were not yet ready, on 22 September 1940 the first tests were made at Rechlin under tow by an He 111. Paul Bader piloted the aircraft: an able man and good test pilot.

Although I was no longer at Heinkel's, in the autumn of 1940 Udet allowed me – certainly because of my experience – to take part in an RLM conference called to discuss the He 280. I arrived late, having been delayed by bad weather, and found that Udet had delivered his own 'blind-flying practice' using a schnapps glass (see Armand van Ishoven: *Udet*, Paul Neff Verlag, Vienna, 1977, page 427):

> Warsitz came soon after to a conference on the He 280 in Berlin. Because of fog his landing at Tempelhof was delayed, Udet receiving him with the words: "What happened to you then? You had your instrument panel with blind-flying equipment, and when the weather closed in, you couldn't land." When his adjutant asked what the Herr *Generaloberst* would do in similar circumstances, he replied: "Quite simple. I fill my schnapps glass and place it forward on the instrument panel. So long as none spills over the rim, the aircraft is flying level." When the adjutant pointed out that the glass would not stay full long, he received the answer: "You beginner. I keep the bottle nearby to refill it."

In this conference, from which industry was excluded, I pointed out amongst other things the difficulties we had experienced after Hitler told me that the 18 months required for the He 178 was too long and the whole project would come too late. I was to be proved right, some years later. When enemy bombers held the skies over Germany and there was a shortage of fighters, the jet programme received the highest priority, but too late. The maiden flight of the He 280 under its own power was made on 30 March 1941 at Marienehe piloted by Fritz Schäfer. The He-S8A turbines on this flight were unjacketed. This was the first ever flight by an aircraft powered by two jet turbines. On 5 April 1941 Bader made an exhibition flight for Udet, Lucht, Reidenbach, Eisenlohr and others, and following this display the achievements of Heinkel were recognized by RLM: rather than have him manufacture both aircraft and turbine at Rostock he was given the Hirth Motoren Werke at Stuttgart. For this recognition Heinkel was indebted principally to Udet.

At the time Messerschmitt was working on the Me 262, which

The He 280 on the first flight by a twin jet turbine powered aircraft on 30 March 1941.

Fritz Wendel test flew for the first time at Leipheim on 18 July 1942. The aircraft had difficulty lifting off because the elevator was ineffective at low speed and the pilot had briefly to touch the brakes to bring the aircraft horizontal for take-off.

I flew the He 280 at Rostock and Berlin on several occasions for research purposes. There were vibrations at the tail and the design lacked a pronounced supersonic wing profile. The Me 262, which I also flew, was not yet ideal: it was improved later and, especially when fitted with Jumo 004 turbines, was superior to the He 280 in every respect, although this was not the factor which decided the RLM in favour of the Me 262.

At RLM and Heinkel, it was said that Heinkel was going downhill, for some time before the maiden flight of the He 178 the technical management had changed, and Hertel had been replaced by Lusser. Long before my time Hertel came to Heinkel from DVL as technical director as an extremely capable and competent aeronautical engineer. Then the Heinkel organization had become unbalanced by abnormally fast growth in response to the demands of the new Third Reich. Heinkel no longer devoted himself to the design work which had previously crowned his activities. Thus it was in the nature of the thing that he handed to Hertel the extremely important technical side

All the photos were taken on the 5 April 1941 in the officer's mess at Heinkel's works in Rostock-Marienehe, after the exhibition of the He 280 made by Paul Bader for Udet, Lucht, Eisenlohr, Reidenbach and others.

From the left, Reidenbach, von Ohain, Udet and Heinkel,

In the centre Udet talking to Heinkel, surrounded by Eisenlohr, Schelp, Lusser, Reidenbach and Günter.

From the left, Udet, Heinkel, Lucht, Reidenbach, Lusser, unknown and Eisenlohr.

The first flight of the Me 262 V3 by Fritz Wendel on 18 July 1942 at Leipheim.

of his great concern. For his part, Hertel, with his knowledge and experience, knew how to turn this situation to his own advantage and began to absorb beneath his umbrella certain operations beyond his sphere. Heinkel recognized what was going on too late and the break came swiftly, although without any great remonstrations.

A good shot of the Me 262 V3.

Göring inspects an Me 262-V6 which was the first version with retractable nose landing gear and an ejector seat.

The Me 262 V1 without turbine engines, but with a conventional piston engine Junkers Jumo 210. The aircraft made the first flight to test the Me 262 airframe on 18 April 1941. A very rare photo.

An excellent photo showing the clean lines of the Me 262 V5 with a fixed nose wheel.

To replace Hertel, Heinkel now brought aboard a man who did not fit the usual Heinkel mould. Everybody was used to the rough but hearty tones of Heinkel, and now came along a sartorially elegant man of 'star allure', sceptre in hand. Lusser came from Messerschmitt where he had a successful track record developing smaller aircraft from the Me 108 to the Me 110. Heinkel's principal interest was in heavy aircraft. Lusser would thus have to adapt and work in an area of expertise to which he was a stranger. Such a situation automatically brought uncertainty. This was tangible and could not be bluffed away with arrogance.

Here I can allow myself to pass judgement based on my personal experiences. Only with the He 280 could Lusser have contributed something positive. I crossed swords with him very soon after he told me how to fly the He 178. Once things got too hot-up I advised him to mind his own business: I had flown satisfactorily so far and would continue to fly as I thought best. He knew that Heinkel rated me highly and so refrained from waging outright war or trying to get me sacked. When I left the firm I discussed with Heinkel the problems I had had with Lusser. I told Heinkel that if he persevered with Lusser he would eventually regret it. A year later when I met Heinkel at Maxim's in Paris during my time as an instructor in France he admitted that I had been right about Lusser. In Berlin I heard that Lusser had been fired with one minute's notice. Consequently it was said at RLM that Lusser had successfully held Heinkel's development back two years.

In contrast to Heinkel, Willy Messerschmitt was the decisive ideas man and designer to the end. One of his talents was skilfully to railroad major conferences. To get his own way he had no inhibitions about doctoring the figures. Heinkel on the other hand lacked diplomatic skill and would quickly hit the roof under pressure, as I witnessed several times at RLM conferences. This was probably the reason for his oft-cited aversion to the RLM, and of them for him. Therefore some at RLM used the temporary disapproval of Heinkel to swing the decision in favour of Messerschmitt. Though Udet was a close friend of Heinkel, he could not always shelter him. After Udet's suicide on 17 November 1941, it followed that Milch should eventually close the books on the He 280 in March 1943*.

---

*In the summer of 1943, RLM invited manufacturers to submit designs for a light jet fighter. Heinkel designed a simple jet monoplane with an He S011 turbine mounted on the roof of the fuselage. This was the future He 162 Volksjäger. After RLM had been absorbed into the Armaments Staff, in October 1944 Heinkel received the first orders to build 1000 machines even before the first prototype had flown. It was intended that the He 162 should become the standard single-engine jet fighter of the Luftwaffe, but the chaotic conditions in Germany during the last year of war ensured that only a handful were operational by the close.

CHAPTER EIGHTEEN

Capitulation and
Siberia

While I was a test pilot my considerable earnings were credited into my bank account. I had no idea what was in the account nor in my wallet, for I needed cash only to buy cigarettes, everything else was found for me as I was working day and night. I knew of course that I could not be a test pilot all my life, and I had to reckon daily with the possibility of pushing up daisies tomorrow. I was already aware of a deterioration in my health through lack of sleep and irregular mealtimes. I was kept under observation by the best medical specialists available who subjected me to regular checks and used me as a medical guinea pig for all manner of tests.

At the outbreak of war I invested some of my money into our family firm 'Feinmechanische Werkstätten' in Berlin so that when the day came and I could no longer fly or do especially useful work I would turn my back on it all and dedicate myself to the business. And as it so happened, in 1942 during a test flight with an Me 109 I had an accident – caused by a faulty fuel lead – which put me out of flying for a year. Thus I took over the management of my father's business and the money left over I put into the 'Warsitz Werke' in Amsterdam making various high-precision materials. On the basis of my experience in the sphere of rocketry, my technical interest and my earlier work with Wernher von Braun, I was involved there in the manufacture of some parts of the A-4 rocket.

As the war situation deteriorated for Germany, in 1943 the Armaments Staff gave me contracts to series-produce valves and parts of the combustion chamber for the A-4, which had received the highest category of priority. My father's business in Berlin was destroyed by Allied bombing in 1943. After the Normandy landings the following year, Warsitz Werke was relocated on the instructions of OKH from Amsterdam to Fürstlich Drehna/ Crinitz – to a contingency location set up in 1943 – and to Nossen. Once reinstated, the Dutch Government impounded the Amsterdam works as an enemy possession. Production by the two factories at Drehna and Nossen was never sizeable since the collapse of the Reich was imminent and communications, particularly the Reich railway system, were a priority target for the enemy, and I lost all contact with my managers through the partial or total disruption of the telephone network.

It is a dreadful period to look back on. The war took on a peculiar form and Hitler's leadership became the purest madness. The worst was the deportation of the Jews: I had many working for me in Amsterdam and when I received the deportation orders I was able to help many by giving them 'indispensable for the work' status. I employed others intentionally in the hope of offering them protection. Money was the decisive factor. I could help many, but not in all cases and not all the time, and I had to be very cautious, for the Gestapo was present everywhere and always!

The work at Nossen was placed under Soviet control after they took over, and for a short while the factory was used exclusively for the production of spare parts for their vehicles. One night the entire works was dismantled and shipped to the Soviet Union. The same happened at Fürstlich Drehna, the standing buildings all being demolished to their foundations. Two days before the Russians arrived I left my principal home at Drehna for Berlin-Klein Machnow where I experienced the capitulation. Shortly before Berlin was divided up into sectors I moved into the American sector in Zehlendorf-West at Himmelsteig 1, where friends put an unoccupied house at my disposal.

I had not availed myself of the opportunity shortly before the capitulation to make for the West because I was hoping to save something of my two businesses in the Eastern Zone once the war ended. Therefore I went to ground in Berlin and at first had no further contact with my factories. As events unfolded I realized in June 1945 the hopelessness of the situation and decided to flee to the West.

Walking to the River Elbe I was captured twice in police raids, once in a private house, the other I was put into a camp in a wood but found it easy to escape. As the Elbe was a military protected area and could not be crossed I headed back to Nossen, where I arranged a secret rendezvous with my former head of personnel, a broken man. He informed me that the Russian *Kommandantur* was anxious to capture me. In the many interrogations of the few employees who had stayed, it was emphasized that I would not be placed under arrest: only my industrial activities and experience in rocketry interested them. I should work for the Russians, he advised.

Next morning news of my presence seemed to have filtered through, for interpreter Braun, a Baltic German who lived in the office house, advised me to flee at once because he knew from the *Kommandantur* that I was going to be arrested. I went immediately to Rosswein, about 30 kilometres from Nossen, to the Ebro Werke, a subsidiary of the light metal smelting works Broer of Hagen-Haspe. The manager, Herr Schüren, was from the main works. I had built this subsidiary myself for the exclusive purpose of manufacturing high-precision parts for my Nossen factory. Schüren knew the danger I was in and arranged for a lorry to take me back to Berlin. He was able to do this because Ebro Werke was now working for the Soviets. I knew that my Nossen factory held nothing more for me, and I could guess what might lay in store for me should I be captured by the Russians, particularly so since in 1944 the Armaments Staff had foisted several hundred forced labourers from the East into my factory.

All the same, in September 1945 I took a chance and went to Drehna again. My brother had a room there with Senior Forester Löbnitz while my aged father lived in his barn. My brother recounted incessant interrogations. In fact, all these interrogations were about me, and he advised me to leave the region at once. That same day I was captured by the Soviets.

I was hauled to my former house on the factory boundary where the GPU had set up its headquarters. The cellars bulged with arrested Germans, the Russian soldiery was in the garages. The factory itself had been reduced to rubble. The bungalows and two-storey houses built for my senior staff had been converted into a Russian field hospital. In my former living room I was brought before a Major, the GPU commander, who advised me through an interpreter that he had orders to send me to the GPU main centre at Frankfurt/Oder. He asked a few questions about the construction method used for some of the works installations which he found suspicious. Finally he wanted to know why I had stowed a bomb on the terrace roof of my house. After he showed it to me, I told him that it was not a bomb but a water heater. He had never seen such a thing before. When I indicated all the taps on hand to supply hot water if the current was up and running he asked if I could fix it. Seeing this as a possible opportunity for escape I agreed.

With a relatively light guard of two men I investigated the possibility of restoration work and established that 3 kilometres of power line had to be replaced. The electric pumps located in a bunker in the works grounds and which had supplied the whole factory with water were still in place. I informed the Major of this and gave him my conditions: I needed electrical current and my brother's help. Once the current was laid on provisionally within two days, my brother and I began work.

Just before it was finished I fled. At night and in fog, on foot or sometimes riding a coal train I got to Berlin relatively easily. Meanwhile my brother got the installation working. For some reason he was not punished in connection with my escape. I guessed that the Major probably had not reported my capture to his superiors, in the long run he created the opportunity himself for my flight.

After these experiences I decided it was best to hide myself away in my West Berlin flat. Wernher von Braun was being held prisoner by the Americans at this time in Bavaria, and he succeeded in sending a courier to contact me in Berlin, but the man was picked up. After that the Americans came for me themselves. A high-ranking officer interviewed me at their HQ. This interrogation was very gentlemanly.

They invited me to work for them, wanted me to be ready immediately, I would be taken to Bavaria and then to the United States. I asked the officer for three days to put my personal affairs in Berlin in order. After much consultation he agreed, putting me on my word of honour.

On the night of 5 December 1945 I was kidnapped from my flat in the American sector of Berlin by four Soviet officers and taken to Berlin-Teltow prison at the barrel of a machine-gun. Thus I vanished, and nobody knew where, including the Americans. From that day on my life was a misery. For weeks on end I endured interrogations every night and was shuttled four times between jails until I finished up in the camp at Hohenschönhausen and a few months later at Sachsenhausen. The innumerable interrogations focused on my Party membership and industrial activities, but the main point of interest was my work on rocket and jet aircraft at OKH and RLM, at Peenemünde and the Heinkel Works. The East, Peenemünde and Rostock being in Russian hands, my former activities were no longer a secret.

At first I was *persona grata* in the jails until I refused to sign a contract which would have obliged me to cooperate for five years on the Russian development in rockets and jets – with an alleged flat in Moscow, 6.500 roubles monthly upkeep, etc. etc. It was obvious to me that having witnessed all the things they were up to I would never see my home again. For my refusal I was declared *persona non grata* and given a medieval third degree in water baths and steam bunkers. At the end of 1946 when I declined the final ultimatum to sign the work contract within three days I was given 25 years' forced labour and shipped out to the notorious punishment camp 7525/13 in Siberia. We travelled in virtually open rail waggons in temperatures of minus 40°C. Every day there were deaths in the waggons. The bodies were thrown into the snow. After a 35-day long journey with little to eat we arrived in a weakened state in Siberia. There I was put to work in two Soviet armaments factories working initially an 18-hour day. When each night we prisoners returned exhausted and hungry to the camp, shadowed by wolves, there was not infrequently a fight to the death over a slice of bread. Although the Russians themselves had little to

СОЮЗ ОБЩЕСТВ
КРАСНОГО КРЕСТА и КРАСНОГО ПОЛУМЕСЯЦА
СССР

ПОЧТОВАЯ КАРТОЧКА ВОЕННОПЛЕННОМУ
Carte postale au prisonnier de guerre

Бесплатно
Franc de port

Кому (Destinataire) ....
Robert Warsitz

Куда (Adresse) **Berlin-Zehlendorf-West**
(страна, город, улица, № дома, округ, село, деревня)
Himmelsteig 1

Отправитель (Expéditeur)
Фамилия и имя отправителя
Nom de l'expéditeur
Erich Warsitz

Почтовый адрес отправителя
Adresse de l'expéditeur
UdSSR   Lager 7525/13

Prière d'écrire sur carte postale, autrement ces lettres ne seront pas remises au destinataire.
Lettre au verso.
T-3, 6. IX—1946 г.

A Message sent from Siberia.

9.XI.48. Liebste Mütz, all meine Lieben! Wiedermal ein
Lebenszeichen + immer noch von hier. Nach den vielen Grüssen
zum 18.X. habe ich keine Nachricht mehr bekommen. Ich hoffe
aber, dass es Euch allen nach wie vor zeitentsprechend
gut geht, — was ich von mir auch sagen kann. Noch habe
ich die Hoffnung nicht ganz aufgegeben, aber sollte ich
Weihnachten immer noch nicht bei Euch sein, so dürft Ihr,
— genau wie ich — nicht verzagen. Ich wünsche Euch allen
besonders den Kleinen, ein frohes Fest. In Gedanken werde
ich bei Euch sein. Ja, man ist hart geworden — das ist
z.Z. gut so! — Vater, was machst Du? Fein, dass es Sybille
besser geht. — Ich freue mich, dass Ihr alle auf dem Bild
unverändert gut ausseht. Liebste Mütz, Kopf hoch, ein-
mal komme ich! — Allen viele liebe Grüsse + Küssings von
Eurem Erich. Auch bitte Frau Schütz küßt T. Fann. usw.

eat, their people in Siberia would often roll a few potatoes or an onion to us under the fence.

A few years later our star amongst the factory-Russians began to rise, for we were improvisers who knew how to make something out of nothing: we made lampshades as barter for a bucket of potatoes. What a luxury! The Russians had developed a soft spot for me and I was able to take advantage of this to obtain lighter work in the laundry, where the inmates included a well-known Wagner female opera singer. And so we sang until the cows came home.

Confirmation of the rightness of my decision not to work for the Russians in their rocket programme came a couple of years before my release. At the end of 1949 or so five German engineers, some of whom had worked for Junkers, were sent to Stalinsk when close to completing their five-year contracts. These people told me that all the

promises were mere window dressing. They received neither adequate remuneration nor correct treatment nor proper sustenance. Their families had been allowed to come but were forced to live with ten other families on one floor of a former children's home in Moscow without enough food or money to clothe the children. Shortly before the contracts expired they were all accused of having sabotaged the Soviet armaments industry, sentenced without trial to 25 years' forced labour and sent to Stalinsk. This was all done for fear that these Germans, on their return to the West, would describe what they had seen in the Soviet Union.

Siberia was a punishment camp for internal exiles, convicted criminals and German PoWs. In the armaments factories

Erich upon his return from Siberia in 1950.

in which I worked I met only Russian exiles. We were all hoping for the next war as our only hope of freedom. Even here I was subjected to constant interrogations. In 1949 a Russian general told me

CONTROL FORM D.2
Kontrollblatt D.2

CERTIFICATE OF DISCHARGE
Entlassungschein

I
PERSONAL PARTICULARS
Personalbeschreibung

ALL ENTRIES WILL BE MADE IN BLOCK LATIN CAPITALS AND WILL BE MADE IN INK OR TYPESCRIPT.

Dieses Blatt muss in folgender weise ausgefüllt werden:
1. In lateinischer Druckschrift und in grossen Buchstaben.
2. Mit Tinte oder mit Schreibmaschine.

SURNAME OF HOLDER *WARSITZ*
Familienname des Inhabers

CHRISTIAN NAMES *ERICH*
Vornamen des Inhabers

DATE OF BIRTH *18.10.06*
Geburtsdatum (DAY/MONTH/YEAR) Tag (Monat/Jahr)

PLACE OF BIRTH *HATTINGEN*
Geburtsort

CIVIL OCCUPATION *FLUG-KAPITAEN*
Beruf oder Beschäftigung

FAMILY STATUS—SINGLE ~~Ledig~~
Familienstand MARRIED Verheiratet
WIDOW(ER) ~~Verwitwet~~
DIVORCED ~~Geschieden~~

HOME ADDRESS Strasse *10*
Heimatanschrift Ort *UFFELN*
Kreis *MINDEN*
Regierungsbezirk/Land
VETMOLV

NUMBER OF CHILDREN WHO ARE MINORS
Zahl der minderjährigen Kinder *2*

I HEREBY CERTIFY THAT TO THE BEST OF MY KNOWLEDGE AND BELIEF THE PARTICULARS GIVEN ABOVE ARE TRUE.
I ALSO CERTIFY THAT I HAVE READ AND UNDERSTOOD THE "INSTRUCTIONS TO PERSONNEL ON DISCHARGE" (CONTROL FORM D.1).
SIGNATURE OF HOLDER
Unterschrift des Inhabers

Ich erkläre hiermit, nach bestem Wissen und Gewissen, dass die obigen Angaben wahr sind.
Ich bestätige ausserdem dass ich die "Anweisung für Soldaten und Angehörige Militär-ähnlicher Organisationen" u.s.w. (Kontrollblatt D.1) gelesen und verstanden habe.

II
MEDICAL CERTIFICATE
Ärztlicher Befund

DISTINGUISHING MARKS *MEN SURNARBEN* †
Besondere Kennzeichen

DISABILITY, WITH DESCRIPTION
Dienstunfähigkeit, mit Beschreibung

— FIT —

MEDICAL CATEGORY
Tauglichkeitsgrad

I CERTIFY THAT TO THE BEST OF MY KNOWLEDGE AND BELIEF THE ABOVE PARTICULARS RELATING TO THE HOLDER ARE TRUE AND THAT HE IS NOT VERMINOUS OR SUFFERING FROM ANY INFECTIOUS OR CONTAGIOUS DISEASE.

Ich erkläre hiermit, nach bestem Wissen und Gewissen, dass die obigen Angaben wahr sind, dass der Inhaber ungezieferfrei ist und dass er keinerlei ansteckende oder übertragbare Krankheit hat.

SIGNATURE OF MEDICAL OFFICER
Unterschrift des Sanitätsoffiziers

NAME AND RANK OF MEDICAL OFFICER IN BLOCK LATIN CAPITALS
Zuname/Vorname/Dienstgrad des Sanitätsoffiziers
(In lateinischer Druckschrift und in grossen Buchstaben)

Flüchtlingslager
Friedland
Der leitende Arzt

P.T.O.
Bitte wenden

† DELETE THAT WHICH IS INAPPLICABLE
Nichtzutreffendes durchstreichen

PSS 2324 6.46 500m

Discharge papers.

... *100,* ' Inti und Bekler

lungsbeihilfe heute gezahlt.

Minden, den 29. 8. 19 50   **III**   ... ung Minden

Kreisverwaltung Minden   **PARTICULARS OF DISCHARGE** als ... lehrerbetreuungsstelle

als ... erbetreuungsstelle   Entlassungsvermerk

THE PERSON TO WHOM THE ABOVE PARTICULARS REFER
Die Person auf die sich obige Angaben beziehen

WAS DISCHARGED ON (Date) .... *7. 6. 50.* .... **FROM THE** *WEHRMACHT SELSE*
wurde am (Datum der Entlassung)   vom/von der   entlassen

RIGHT THUMBPRINT	
Abdruck des rechten Daumens	

CERTIFIED BY
Beglaubigt durch

OFFICIAL

NAME, RANK AND   J. Wood. R. S. M.
APPOINTMENT OF   2 P.W. Discharge Centre
ALLIED DISCHARGING   Amtlicher
OFFICER IN   Einprägestempel
BLOCK CAPITALS,

EMBOSSED SEAL

Flüchtlingslager
Friedland/Leine

(W. DISCHARGE CENTRE No. 2)

INSERT "ARMY", "NAVY", "AIR FORCE", "VOLKSSTURM", OR PARA-MILITARY
ORGANIZATION, e.g. "R.A.D.", "N.S.F.K.", ETC.
Wehrmachtteil oder Gliederung der die Einheit angehört, z.B. "Heer", "Kriegsmarine",
"Luftwaffe", "Volkssturm", "Waffen SS" oder "R.A.D." "N.S.F.K.", u.s.w.

... W. 3. 5. 1950.

40.– DM PAID ON DISCHARGE

SIGNED

PAYMASTER

DM ....
erhalten zu haben bescheinigt.

Minden, den .... 195...

M *300. –* .... Entl.- und Beklei-
dungsbeihilfe heute gezahlt.

Minden, den 11. Juli 19 50

Kreisverwaltung Minden

Kreiskasse Minden

Discharge papers.

personally that I would never see my homeland again. Although that same year I was convicted by a flying court of decisive collaboration in an illegal weapon of war on 6 April 1950 I was shipped out to Frankfurt/Oder with the last transport. After many years of captivity, most former Wehrmacht prisoners were freed on the intervention of Federal Chancellor Konrad Adenauer.

The march from the station to the Frankfurt/Oder interrogation camp was guarded by East Germans and it was quite easy to melt away. I made my way westwards through wood and meadow. One day, desperately hungry and weak, I came to a cottage where an old widow lived. She had almost nothing for herself but gave me a little bread and milk. She told me she had lost both her sons in the war, provided me with a pistol and said, 'Make sure you get back to freedom with it!' I thanked her from the bottom of my heart and after many days and nights of adventure eventually reached West Berlin, and thus did get back to freedom.

CHAPTER NINETEEN

1951–1982

During the war my father and his brother hoarded gold, which helped me to make a new start in Germany. I had the best contacts to German industry and many friends there helped me, after the war and Siberia, to get back on my feet. The fruits of this was my fine-engineering firm (MH) at Hilden. Those were very difficult years. Often at the beginning I would fall asleep at my desk. Before founding MH I met my good friend Wernher von Braun secretly. He lived in the United States then, and one day phoned inviting me to visit, although warning that I should expect to add an extra notch to my belt, for things were tight there for Germans! Officially, I could not visit. I was refused a visa because my name was blacklisted. After five years in Siberia, the Americans thought I might be a Soviet spy. Instead, I went to Montreal where Dieter Stinnes introduced me to a senior American military officer. Passage was arranged for me aboard ship. In the United States I met Wernher von Braun at a secret location. It was a wonderful day!

It would be many years before our next meeting when he came to Germany to receive the Service Order of the German Federal Republic from the President. Shortly afterwards, on 5 September 1959, he visited me at the MH to commemorate the twentieth anniversary of the world's first rocket-aircraft and jet flights. Another great day for us both!

Towards the end of that year, I spent a long period of convalescence recovering from a heart attack. The sanatorium was at Cademario in southern Switzerland, and as I liked Tessin so much I bought a piece of land there to build a second home. These were my first contacts with the Swiss. Some of the attorneys with whom I was involved during the land purchase were very keen on flying.

In Germany, an American concern offered to buy the MH at

Wernher von Braun and Erich.

Wernher von Braun, Hugo Stinnes and Erich.

1959: Wernher von Braun views a painting of the He 178.

Hilden to set up an aircraft parts production factory and install me as General Manager. Until then I had made a good living, but the offer was well worth considering, especially since I would be in contact with the world of aircraft once more. The price was very good, and so in 1962 I accepted the offer. Unfortunately, they never produced aircraft parts there. This disappointed me, and in 1964 I resigned. At that time I was strengthening my ties with Switzerland. A Swiss firm offered to build me a hangar on the small airfield at Agno to overhaul aircraft engines. At the beginning they needed 750 specialists, and later 2,500, but as such people were not to be found in Switzerland, they would have to come from abroad.

In 1964, I began the building of Villa Roncolago, now a representative's home rather than a second residence. The famous architect Orfeo Armado drew up the plans. At the time, this was a sensational project. 100 men were engaged on the work. It took a year to finish the villa, and in August 1965 I emigrated with my family to Switzerland. The hangar project eventually came to nothing, because the Swiss Government would not allow the employment of foreigners. I was left with Villa Roncolago on my hands and so I

Dr Bender, Max Meyer and Erich in Switzerland.

1960: Walter Künzel and Erich.

decided to remain in Switzerland, "Alps-side" as we say, with my family – my wife Doris and sons, Lutz and Roby. In subsequent years, I received many visits from friends of the 1930s. A special event was a reunion at the villa with the Peenemünde team of the time: Uwo Pauls, Max Meyer, Dr Bender, Dr Hengst and others. Usually these reunions were held in Germany. On 16 June 1977, we were saddened to learn of the death of Wernher von Braun. We had gone through so much together. My own health was by no means of the best, particularly in 1979/80, but the skill of the doctors and my wife's care helped pull me through.

At the time of writing in 1982, forty-three years have elapsed since the world's first jet flight,

Erich at the time he wrote these memoirs in 1982.

and in the intervening years I have often been asked if I realized at that time that the German rocket and jet test programme would be the decisive step forward. We knew – from our technical espionage service – that the British and Americans had such a project but were not so far advanced as we were. I knew there was nothing similar anywhere in the world, but I was not imagining myself wearing the laurel wreath! All the same I was aware what great advances flights with the He 176 and He 178 would signify, and I was also convinced that within a few years few military and civilian commercial aircraft would still be flying with a piston-engine and propellors. But at that time I was called an incurable optimist!

We were correct in thinking then that we had beaten the world and successfully ushered in a new epoch. We soon sobered up, however,

German aviation pioneers meet at Baden-Baden in 1964. From the left: Dr Ing. Wurster (Messerschmitt), Ernst Seibert (Junkers), Heinz Kindermann (Junkers), Fritz Wendel (Messerschmitt), Gerhard Nitschke (Heinkel) and Erich.

for with the outbreak of war Berlin had other things on its plate and much came to nothing, including my personal ambition of breaking the world speed record with the He 176. That would have crowned the first phase of rocket-propelled flight after all the pioneer work.

Even when Heinkel finally succeeded a few months later in getting Milch, Udet, Lucht and the entire RLM technical staff to Marienehe, and I was able to demonstrate the He 178 in flight after the previous failure at take-off, interest and support was incomprehensibly absent. Quite the contrary: lack of appreciation, difficulties and envy followed. Even the top brass considered the whole thing to be no more than an impressive plaything. Despite all setbacks, however, Heinkel pressed ahead with the work, even when a part of the further development was banned.

It was rather more than an impressive plaything, of course, for after the war it surged ahead by leaps and bounds and time has shown that what we aimed for and proved possible in the first developments and tests has become the reality. Nowadays it is an everyday occurrence to see military and civilian jet aircraft in the skies, able to fly from Frankfurt to New York in six hours.

My wish to experience something revolutionary and sensational came to fruition with the successful moon landing, in which Wernher von Braun played such a decisive role. I often think how the modern space-shuttle resembles the minute He 176, also fired into the air by a rocket, and also glided back down to earth – and wonder what more the future in space holds beyond our present imagination!

When I reflect on my life today, I have to say that the period of the Thirties was the finest and most exciting time of my life. A great dream was realized, flying became my everything, and what I achieved far exceeded what I had thought for myself at the outset. Looking back I am very proud of that and thank my Creator that I am still around to relate a story which is perhaps still of interest. I wish all aviators a safe landing.

Lutz Warsitz

The time passed quickly and soon my father and I had been working on my project for over a year. We wrote and phoned all over the world in our search for more information and I got to know my father as never before. After the interview was basically completed many questions still remained unanswered and everyday more occurred to me once I picked up the threads and continued the research. Unfortunately the questions which he could have answered will now never be. Had he survived then many of my discoveries would have interested him, and he would have enjoyed seeing the films of the He 111, He 112 and the He 178 which have finally come to light with the changes in the political situation and digital archiving!

In April 1983 he was admitted into intensive care and there now began the struggle for life which he lost while in the bosom of the family and at home on 12 July 1983. I am grateful to have the opportunity with this book to honour his memory as one of the great aviation pioneers, as a man and a father. I hope that it will give rise to analysis and discussion enabling us to bridge the gaps in our knowledge and correct errors. New research findings, documents and photographs may eventually surface from the depths of presently sealed archives.

An example is the He 176! Until a few years ago there was no known photograph of this aircraft. Many people asked whether it might not be the figment of somebody's imagination. Of course it existed, but a veil of mystery still surrounds the machine because until today almost nothing is known about it despite the existence – as my father maintained – of crates of film and photographs.

Recently a photograph of the He 176-V1 has come to light, resolving a riddle for me about the nose-wheel. None of those

From the left: Erich's brother Kurt and his sister Bruni, Kurt's wife Mieze, Doris and Erich. Sitting: Erich's father and standing to the right, Erich's young son Lutz.

Erich died on 12 July 1983.

involved at the time, neither my father nor Wernher von Braun, Heinkel or Künzel ever mentioned the He 176 having a nose-wheel. Some while ago another photo (see page 90) appeared in which the aircraft is seen fitted with the enclosed panoramic cockpit. The outline of the nose-wheel is clearly visible in this photograph as well! Was it the purpose of having the nose-wheel to keep the aircraft on a fixed heading on the ground because of the eternal problem experienced at take-off due to the ineffective rudder at low speeds?

As one can see there remains much to be clarified, and I should be grateful for further information, documents, photos or film which would then be included in a reprint of this book and help complete the remainder of the jigsaw in this important pioneering achievement in the history of rocket and jet aircraft development.

The recently discovered photo of the He 176.

INDEX